1,001 Smiles

1,001
Smiles

Marion Kaplinsky

CHRONICLE BOOKS

SAN FRANCISCO

1,001 Smiles
Marion Kaplinsky

First published in the United States in 2005 by Chronicle Books, LLC.

Conceived, created, and designed by Duncan Baird Publishers.

Library of Congress Cataloging-in-Publication Data:
1,001 smiles / [compiled] by Marion Kaplinsky.
      p. cm.
1. American wit and humor. 2. Quotations, English.
I. Title: One thousand one smiles. II. Title: One thousand and one smiles.
III. Kaplinsky, Marion.
  PN6165.A17 2005
  081—dc22
                 2004026435
ISBN 0-8118-4763-2

Manufactured in Thailand

Editor: Zoë Fargher
Managing designer: Manisha Patel
Designer: Justin Ford
Commissioned artwork: Allan Sanders

Typeset in Shannon

Distributed in Canada by Raincoast Books
9050 Shaughnessy Street
Vancouver, British Columbia V6P 6E5

10 9 8 7 6 5 4 3 2 1

Chronicle Books LLC
85 Second Street
San Francisco, California 94105

www.chroniclebooks.com

A smile is a curve that sets
everything straight

INTRODUCTION

We smile when we are happy, when we want to send out a message of love or support, and when we are amused. Sometimes a smile will mean all these different things at once. For example, we are likely to find life's quirks and contradictions especially amusing when we are happy; and, conversely, smiling can enlarge our sense of well-being. Moreover, giving someone support might involve getting them to see the funny side of their situation, or of the ups and downs of fortune, or perhaps of the ways in which other people are behaving toward them.

The idea behind this book is to mix these different kinds of smiles together and offer a collection of smile-makers, some of them reassuring, some of them comic, some of them reminding us of life's blessings. It is the book to reach for when you are feeling a bit low and need cheering up, or, equally, when you are in good form, among good company, and feel like sharing some good-hearted laughter together.

Many of the "smiles" gathered here are jokes, and it is hoped that you will react to at least some of them noisily.

Others are designed to prompt a gentle, perhaps even scarcely perceptible smile of well-being, like the smile of a person who is pleased about some happy secret they are keeping or some windfall that has come their way.

Laughter is mysterious – we all know what it feels like, and how good it feels, but it's difficult for us to understand, even more to explain, exactly how it happens. Our fancy is tickled by something that comes at us from left field – an observation, a joke, an amusing juxtaposition of objects or words, a witty remark – and we react physically, with an involuntary adjustment to muscles in the face, and with a corresponding sensation of release. No one knows why we respond this way, but we enjoy it all the same. Suddenly we switch our attention away from serious or neutral matters and, for a few moments, we relish the unexpected. We glimpse a new horizon, a fresh perspective, something that restores or enlivens our spirits. It's the ultimate stress relief.

Many conventional books of jokes tend toward the cynical, but cynicism is an intensely negative viewpoint, and on the

whole we have avoided it here. A healthy, tolerant scepticism, however, has been exercised with great relish – after all, it's great fun to ridicule human foibles, especially when we are targeting ourselves, or our own social group or gender, as much as others. What better way to correct our inflated ego than to puncture its bubble and make it an object of mirth?

Another common source of laughter, generously represented here, is the application of a child's naïve logic to situations in their lives or to the adult business going on all around them. Children are delightfully and unconsciously amusing in the way they make sense of their adventures and encounters, and many of the children's remarks or questions quoted in this book are indebted to the gentle adult art of eavesdropping. We have also put in some unashamedly silly "smiles" which are borrowed from the wonderful ways that children see the world, but which will delight all ages.

Yet another effective trigger for the release that laughter brings is the surreal – a moment of escape from the laws of everyday reality, whether expressed in word play or in strange scenarios that twist the logic of the actual and manufacture something bizarre from innocent ingredients. Question: "How does the man on the moon get his hair cut?" Answer: "Eclipse it."

Finally, there are many "smiles" here that seek not to amuse, but to console or reassure, with sympathy and warmth; as well as a handful of memorable quotations drawn from many different times and places about the value of laughter or smiling, intended to serve as occasional reminders or to inspire us with their depth of insight or their felicitous phrasing.

And that's probably enough by way of preamble – I had better not keep you waiting to smile any longer. I hope you smile bigtime!

1 **Catch that smile**

We can all get more out of our lives if we avoid building unnecessary fences – work and play belong to the same world, and the possibilities for laughter lie equally within each of them.

2   Lunch logic

If I were given the choice between my heart's desire and a cheese sandwich, I would definitely choose the cheese sandwich. After all, nothing's better than your heart's desire, and a cheese sandwich is better than nothing.

3   Safety first

He who laughs last should do so from a safe distance.

4   Table of equivalents

"One machine can do the work of 50 ordinary men. No machine can do the work of one extraordinary man."

ELBERT HUBBARD (1856–1915)

5   Mantra for the 21st century

Veni, Video, Visa – I came, I saw, I shopped.

6   Practical magic

A little girl said to her dad that she'd like a magic wand for Christmas, and then added, "And don't forget to put the batteries in!"

7   A definition

Modesty: The gentle art of enhancing your charm by pretending not to be aware of it.

8   Sweetness and light

"How much honey can a bee make in a day?"
"Enough to fill one jam jar, with a little bit left over to stick on the label."

9   Accidental hero

"The greatest pleasure I know is to do a good action by stealth and have it found out by accident."

CHARLES LAMB (1775–1834)

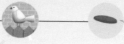

10   Pedal power

Little Johnny: "Mom, please will you buy me a bicycle for my birthday?"

Mom: "Will it make you behave any better if I do?"

Little Johnny: "No, but I'll behave over a wider area."

11   Vow of silence

A man joined an abbey and took a vow of silence: he was allowed to speak only two words every five years. After the first five years had passed, he went to see the abbot and said, "Bed hard." Whereupon he turned around and walked out of the door.

Five years later he went to see the abbot again and said, "Food cold." Again, he turned and walked out.

After another five years had passed, he once more went to see the abbot. This time he said, "I quit."

"I'm not surprised," responded the abbot. "All you've done since you got here is complain."

12   Great news!

"Whoopee!" yelled the blues singer on hearing that
he'd been offered his first record contract. "The only
trouble is, I never felt less like singing the blues!"

13   Out shopping

I went to a bookstore and asked the saleswoman,
"Where's the self-help section?" She wouldn't tell me.
She said it would defeat the whole purpose.

14   Spiritual sustenance

A Buddhist monk walked up to a hot-dog stand.
"Make me one with everything," he said.

15   Savoir faire

"To be agreeable in society you must consent to be
taught things that you already know."

JOHANN KASPAR LAVATER (1741–1801)

16 **Proverbial wisdom**

If a dog's prayers were answered,
bones would fall from the sky.

17   Community of souls

The world is like a beehive: we all enter by the same
door but we live in different cells.

18   Have faith

"Ten thousand difficulties do not make one doubt."

CARDINAL JOHN HENRY NEWMAN (1801–1890)

19   Surprise surprise!

A boy went up to his father with his hands behind his
back and said, "Dad, I have a present for you."

"How nice," said the father. "What is it?"

"A packet of assorted decibels," said the boy as he
produced his harmonica.

20   New broom

Laughter is the brush that sweeps away the cobwebs of
the heart.

21   Ulterior motive

"Always forgive your enemies; nothing annoys them so much."

OSCAR WILDE (1854–1900)

22   Ouch!

A husband and wife went to see a dentist. The husband said, "I want a tooth pulled. I don't want gas or Novocain because I'm in a terrible hurry. Just do it as quickly as possible." "You're a brave man," said the dentist. "Now, show me which tooth it is." So the husband turned to his wife and said, "Open your mouth and show him the tooth!"

23   Down Memory Lane

The older we become, the more zany were our childhood friends and the more outrageous their antics.

24   Egg count

An elderly pastor was searching his closet for his collar before church one Sunday morning. In the back of the closet, he found a small box containing three eggs and 100 $1 bills.

He called his wife and asked her about the box and its contents. Embarrassed, she admitted having hidden the box there for all the 30 years of their marriage: she hadn't told him because she didn't want to hurt his feelings. He asked her how the box could have hurt his feelings. She said that every time during their marriage that he had delivered a poor sermon, she had placed an egg in the box.

The pastor felt that three poor sermons in 30 years was certainly nothing to feel bad about, so he asked her what the $100 was for.

"Each time I got a dozen eggs," she replied, "I sold them to the neighbours for $1."

25 **Open house**

Last night I lay in bed looking up at the stars in the sky and I thought to myself, "Who's stolen my ceiling?"

26 **Rainforest chat**

Two parrots are sitting on a perch. One says to the other, "Can you smell fish?"

27 **Mirror image**

Life is like a mirror. If you frown at it, it frowns back; if you smile, it returns the greeting.

28 **Hats galore**

"Buying a hat is such a difficult business," said the customer to the sales assistant in the men's clothing department of Bloomingdale's. "I really do like this one, but to be absolutely sure I think I'd better audition the band."

29 A breath of fresh air

I love walking in the hills with the wind in my hair and only my appetites and anxieties to keep me company. They're like dogs – take them for a walk from time to time and it stops them barking themselves hoarse and chewing up the carpet.

30 Two's company

We all love company – if only that of a burning candle. When a shy person holds a party, it's best to keep a fire extinguisher handy.

31 Never never

Life is full of surprises. Just say "never" and you'll see.

32 Swedish proverb

Don't throw away the old bucket until you are sure that the new one holds water.

33   Real modesty

"I don't want any of you to make a fuss over me. Just treat me like you would any other great man."

34   Phone pest

A man called the police station to say that he'd been receiving a lot of nuisance phone calls. "Oh, not you again!" they said.

35   Free advice

If you have to borrow money, borrow it from a pessimist – they never expect it back.

36   A prayer

"Lord, lead me not into temptation (I can find the way myself)."

37 **The way of the tiger**
Better for us to have lived for
one day as a tiger than a
thousand years in a pair of
striped pajamas.

38   A question

People are always talking about a credibility gap. But what's supposed to go into it? A gullibility fill?

39   A definition

Lottery: A tax on people who are bad at math.

40   Mouse attack

A man who was very hard up put a picture of a chunk of cheese in his mousetrap, to save money. Next morning, he checked the trap and was pleased to see that it had worked: he'd caught a picture of a mouse.

41   Helping hands

It's great to be alone occasionally but few of us would want to make it a way of life: you can go and find a stranger to help you change a tyre but you can't really ask one to help you change the duvet cover.

42   Larger than life

Our virtues cannot be quantified – that is, unless we have a very powerful magnifying glass.

43   Airwaves

Control to pilot: "What is your height and position?"
Pilot: "I'm five feet eight inches and I'm sitting down."

44   Love thine enemy

"Nobody will ever win the battle of the sexes. There's too much fraternizing with the enemy."
HENRY KISSINGER (b.1923)

45   Lost in translation

A little language can be a dangerous thing. In the early days of computer translation, "Out of sight, out of mind", translated into Russian and then back to English, became "Invisible maniac".

46 **An everyday miracle**

Anyone can discover a million miracles in a single day. There are three steps to this. First, consider the miracle of technology. Next, dwell on the fact that technology cannot reproduce a single blade of grass. Then comes the last step: find a lawn.

47   **Magnolia Lane**

Suburbia: Where they tear out the trees and then name streets after them.

48   **Nursery knowledge**

"An unbreakable toy is useful for breaking other toys."
SAMUEL, AGED 7

49   **Retail therapy**

First lady: "Whenever I'm down in the dumps, I buy myself a new hat."
Second lady: "Oh, so that's where you get them?"

50   **Experiment**

Try typing with your nose. Chances are that what you write won't make much sense, but you'll never take your fingers for granted again.

51   The law of human dynamics

If everything's under control, you're moving too slowly.

52   Royal pronouncement

"Anger makes dull men witty, but it keeps them poor."

ELIZABETH I (1533–1603)

53   Mind over matter

Only try to undergo major root canal
work without anaesthetic if you
are a Buddhist and can
transcend dental medication.

54   Pure intentions

Never attribute to malice
that which is adequately
explained by stupidity.

55   **Upside down**

It's possible – and usually productive – to view almost everything from a different perspective. Artists do it, exercising the right side of the brain to be creative. You'll notice funny things about familiar objects. A pair of legs, for example: the bottom is actually at the top.

56   **Fair point**

If I were two-faced, why would I wear this one?

57   **Under a spell**

Man to woman: "I'm under hypnosis, and I've been ordered to kiss the first pretty girl I see."

Woman to man: "I'm under hypnosis too, and I'm a man-eating tiger drawn to you by the smell of peanut butter on your shirt-cuffs."

58 **Late extras**

Afterthoughts are often more significant than the thoughts that prompted them.

59 **Helpless**

Sometimes we know what the solution is but find ourselves unable to put it into practice – like a dentist with toothache camping alone in the Catskills.

60 **In the balance**

"An ounce of loyalty is worth a pound of cleverness."
ELBERT HUBBARD (1856–1915)

61 **Fooling ourselves**

Seeking advice isn't the same as looking for an answer. We already know the answer, but we seek advice because we wish we didn't.

62 Fairytale ending?

The teddy bears' picnic was going very well – until
Goldilocks came along with their homework.

63 Let him be

"Do not free a camel of the burden of his hump; you
may be freeing him from being a camel."

G.K. CHESTERTON (1874–1936)

64 Not my fault

He who cannot dance blames the band for being
under-rehearsed.

POLISH PROVERB

65 Downside

A bird in the hand might well be worth two in the
bush, but it makes blowing your nose very difficult.

66 **A stretch too far**

If God meant us to touch our toes, he would have put them higher up our body.

67   **Who's who**

"Who is the world's most prominent Zen teacher?"
"M.T. Ness."

68   **Self-reliance**

God provides a worm for every bird – but he doesn't
lay it out in the nest like a surprise birthday gift.

69   **The appliance of science**

Animal testing is a terrible idea – they get all nervous
and give you the wrong answers.

70   **Look on the bright side**

If you've been sacked from every job you ever had, at
least no one can call you a quitter.

71   **Proverbial wisdom**

A closed mouth gathers no foot.

72   Humble pie

Always use tasteful words – you never know when you'll have to eat them.

73   True happiness

"We act as though comfort and luxury were the chief requirements of life, when all we need to make us really happy is something to be enthusiastic about."

CHARLES KINGSLEY (1819–1875)

74   Risk assessment

If at first you don't succeed, skydiving is not for you.

75   Left and right

The right brain is the source of inspiration, the left brain the seat of reason. That's why inspired people always think they're right and reasonable people get left out in the cold.

A question of physics

If boomerangs come back to you
when you throw them,
why don't bananas?

77   Tightwad

I never lend money when there's a y in the day.

78   Encouragement

Remember the Tokyo mailman on his first day at work: things can only get easier.

79   Wise words

"Depend upon it, if a man talks of his misfortunes there is something in them that is not disagreeable to him; for where there is nothing but pure misery, there never is any recourse to the mention of it."

SAMUEL JOHNSON (1709–1794)

80   The heart of the matter

A life without worldly ambition is like a fish without a snorkel.

81　Spanish proverb

Mañana is often the busiest day of the week.

82　A good listener

A friend is someone who hears the song in our heart
and tells us honestly that we're singing out of key.

83　Mail check

An old lady was sending her family a large Bible.
"Is there anything breakable in this package, ma'am?"
asked the mailman.
"Only the Ten Commandments," she said.

84　Proverbial wisdom

Believe those who seek the truth,
but doubt those who find it.

85   Older and braver

"I speak truth, not so much as I would, but as much as
I dare; and I dare a little more, as I grow older."

MICHEL DE MONTAIGNE (1533–1592)

86   Life lesson

If you can't be a good example, be a terrible warning.

87   Food facts

Hunger is the best sauce. Tomato ketchup comes a
close second.

88   Looking for the light

Many of us look for the meaning of life in worldly
things, such as careers, material possessions and
luxuries of all kinds. We might as well stand with an
electric flashlight on the west coast of Ireland and hope
to illuminate the Statue of Liberty.

89 Storm warning

"Marriage may often be a stormy lake, but celibacy is almost always a muddy horsepond."

THOMAS LOVE PEACOCK (1785–1866)

90 Prizewinner

"Why did the farmer, the scarecrow and the theoretical physicist share the Nobel Prize?"

"They were all outstanding in their fields."

91 A wager

President Calvin Coolidge was famous for being sparing with his words: he only spoke when he had to.

At an official dinner in Washington a woman went up to him and said with a smile: "Mr President, I've made a bet that I can get you at say at least three words to me."

"You lose," said Coolidge.

92 Best of both

Be modest – and proud of it!

93 First impressions

"If you want to find out your true opinion of anybody, just notice the impression made on you the first time you receive a letter from them."

ARTHUR SCHOPENHAUER (1788–1860)

94 Confidential

Don't pay any attention to what they say about you – it's what they whisper that's important.

95 Country living

Some people live so deep in the country that they can be miles from the nearest cappuccino machine. By the time they get home with their coffee the froth's given up the ghost entirely.

96   Over the top

Exaggeration is a hundred, million, billion times worse than understatement.

97   Turning a corner

Two wrongs don't make a right, but three lefts do.

No excuse

A survey of attitudes among children has shown that dogs are by far the most popular pets – no doubt because claiming that the goldfish ate your homework would stretch credulity a little too far.

99   Samples

The greatness of a great writer cannot be proven by
selective quotations. It would be like putting your
house up for sale and carrying a brick in your pocket
to show potential buyers.

100   Testing

"In examinations those who do not wish to know ask
questions of those who cannot tell."

SIR WALTER ALEXANDER RALEIGH (1861–1922)

101   Deep distinction

Philosophy is to faith as a sundial is to a Swiss watch.

102   Wholly absorbed

"Man is most nearly himself when he achieves the
seriousness of a child at play."

HERACLITUS (540–480BC)

103   Indulge yourself

If something is worth doing, it's worth overdoing.

104   Our destiny

The three ages of birdman: fledgling, night owl and homing pigeon.

105   Christmas blues

"Why was Santa's little helper depressed?"
"He had low elf-esteem."

106   Wise choice

If you are unable to decide between two alternatives, choose that for which you retain the receipt.

107   Uncharted territory

When we're lost in thought, could the reason be that we're on totally unfamiliar terrain?

108 One plus three

It's easy to apportion blame to someone else. You just point a finger at them. But have you ever noticed where the other three are pointing when you do that?

109 Lucky Adam!

"What a good thing Adam had. When he said a good thing he knew nobody had said it before."

MARK TWAIN (1835–1910)

110 Special privilege

Loneliness is a misunderstanding. It's simply God wanting a private word with you.

111 Roadworks

Seek out the road to success, but don't be surprised if you find it's still under construction.

112   Last chance

A man is sitting on the couch holding the TV remote
control. He shouts to his wife, who's in the kitchen:
"Hey, Mary. Is there anything you need to say to me
before the football season starts?"

113   Wrong volume

Steer clear of a "self-help" book called *How to Hug*. It's
actually Volume IX of the Encyclopedia Britannica.

114   Hmmmm

"Why do bees hum?"
"Because they've forgotten the words."

115   Time out

Sleep is when the real you takes a break from your
personality.

116 **Gambling on love**

The French say, "il m'aime un peu, beaucoup, à la folie, pas du tout."
(He loves me a little, a lot, madly, not at all.)
That gives better odds than "loves me, loves me not".

117 Brave explorer

As a child I was greatly inspired by a globe of the world that sat on the desk in my father's study. It was then that I conceived my great ambition – to travel. In later life, in my early twenties, I finally realized this ambition, setting off alone in search of the seam.

118 A stranger in our midst

You all laugh at me because I am different. But I laugh at you because you are all the same.

119 No answer

You know, God does visit us. A lot. It's just that most of the time we're not at home.

120 Weather alert

Rain is nature's way of warning us of low-flying clouds.

121 Shades of gray

Sometimes we're just too black and white in our thinking instead of acknowledging shades of gray. The world can't always be neatly parcelled up in the way that some of our questions about life might imply. That's why, instead of asking for "answers" in a math test, they should just ask for "impressions".

122 Swedish proverb

Fear less, hope more; eat less, chew more; whine less, breathe more; talk less, say more; hate less, love more; and all good things are yours.

123 Don't bother

"Never explain – your friends do not need it and your enemies will not believe you anyway."

ELBERT HUBBARD (1856–1915)

124 **Cupid on the warpath**

First little girl:
"Where are you going
with that bow and arrow?"
Second little girl:
"I'm going next door to make
Johnny fall in love with me."

125   What are you saying?

Every present carries a subliminal message, they say.
When a father gives his son a train set, it's a
subconscious nostalgia for the railroads of his youth.
So why has my wife given me a cactus in a pot for
the windowsill?

126 **A word from the wise**

"I always pass on good advice. It is the only thing to do with it. It is never of any use to oneself."

OSCAR WILDE (1854–1900)

127 **Ambient music**

A birth these days is as carefully planned as a wedding. The expectant mother interviews midwives, chooses fresh flowers for her bedside table, and selects soothing music to accompany the contractions – perhaps one of the many fine compositions written for the pandemonium.

128 **Comic opera**

I went to see Pavarotti sing once. It was wonderful, but I'll tell you something – he doesn't like it much if you join in.

129 Retrace your steps

Our best chance of finding God is to look in the place where we left him.

130 Know the difference

In youth, the absence of pleasure is a pain; but in old age, the absence of pain is a pleasure.

131 Advice for travellers

Tune into the rhythm of life, but don't ever get your speedometer confused with your clock, because the faster you go the later you'll think you are.

132 **Detective**

A mother came across her little boy looking through his grandmother's jewelry box. Holding up the jewels, he announced with a look of surprise:

"I think Granny's a burglar!"

133   Perfect partners

There are quite a lot of advantages to being single, but there comes a time when you long for the companionship of another being, one who will treat you with adoration, who will be kind and faithful when times are hard, who will share your joys and sorrows. Time, then, to buy a puppy.

134   A simple life

Buddhists have no attachments – which can make it very difficult for them to vacuum under the couch.

135 Living with fear

Anxiety is only a problem if you decide it's a problem. Make it a companion instead. Take it on vacation with you. Have it round for a meal. It's only when it doesn't send you a thank-you note that there's really any cause for concern.

136 Hindsight

A man of 90 was asked to what he attributed his longevity. His reply was, "It's probably because most nights I went to bed and slept when I should have sat up and worried."

137 Abstinence

Give up carnal relations and you will live longer, certain mystics claim. Actually, you may not, but it will probably feel like it.

138 **The bright side**
Why is common sense like
a rainbow? Because it
never appears until
the storm is over.

139 **Proverbial wisdom**
Never cross a bridge until
you come to it.

140   Change for the better

Trouble with boundaries has a long history. Back in the bad old days, a group of Russian surveyors was charged with drawing the definitive border between Poland and the USSR. On a farm up to then regarded as in Belarus, they told the farmer that the maps were wrong and that his land was in Poland. "Thank God!" said the farmer, "I couldn't stand another Russian winter."

141   What a giveaway!

"That's a fine essay for someone of your age," said the teacher to the pupil. "How about someone of my Mom's age?" came the reply.

142   Proverbial wisdom

Every time a sheep bleats it misses a nibble.

143   Body language

They say that you can cross any bridge with enough perseverance. But they're wrong. You can't cross the bridge of your nose.

144   Heavy weather

March is an overspill for the foul weather February couldn't fit into its schedule.

145   Someone cares

If you think nobody cares if you're alive or dead, try missing a couple of mortgage payments.

146   Trouble in the Post Office

"'I'll have that one, please,' he said, pointing to the middle of the sheet of stamps."

SIR HERBERT BEERBOHM TREE (1853–1917)

147 **The Fountain of Youth**

"Whatever a man's age may be, he can reduce it several years by putting a bright-coloured flower in his buttonhole."

MARK TWAIN (1835–1910)

148 **Dirty chicken**

"Why did the chicken cross the road, roll in the dirt, and cross the road again?"

"Because he was a dirty double crosser."

149 **A question of taste**
"What garlic is to salad,
insanity is to art."
AUGUSTUS HOMER SAINT-GAUDENS
(1848–1907)

150 **Instant self-esteem**
When you're suffering from
low self-esteem, just phone
yourself. The line will always be
busy. See? People like you.
You're popular.

151 **A living contradiction**
All of us are a blend of
fools and angels. We rush
in and fear to tread at the
same time.

152   Natural wisdom

The woods provide great schooling for a child. You can learn about the birds and the bees, the weather, the rhythms of nature, and two difficult words: "Trespassers" and "prosecuted".

153   Left until last

"Why was Adam created on the sixth day, after all the other creatures?"

"So that if a person ever becomes puffed up with pride, he could be reminded that the amoeba, the slug and the worm preceded him in the order of creation."

154   Vegetable power

With children, the carrot works better than the stick. Except, of course, when you're trying to get them to eat their carrots.

155   Starting young

Children often do quite wonderful paintings, which are not properly appreciated only because they are not presented professionally, as abstract art, in a frame, in a modern art gallery. Do a deal with your child: get him or her to allow you to claim their best paintings as your own, and give them 0.1 percent of any proceeds you can obtain from an art dealer. This is best attempted before your child learns percentages.

156   Better safe than sorry

Never let your pet see you misbehaving: no one knows precisely how God obtains the information he uses to make his judgments.

157   No Moses

Atheism is a non-prophet-making religion.

158 Fish alert

Talking about self-improvement all the time isn't a very self-improving pastime. It's like looking for fish-prints in a dry riverbed.

159 Time for another

The glass is neither half-empty nor half-full. It's an opportunity for a refill.

160 Zoo time

Little Ben: "Dad, will you take me to the zoo today?"
Ben's Dad: "Certainly not. If they want you, they can come and get you."

161 The pre-treat moment

There's a moment just before you taste something delicious that feels quite a lot better than the tasting that follows.

162   Sleepy hollow

A minute's meditation is worth an hour's sleep. If only someone had told Rip Van Winkle.

163   Four ways of looking at a black sheep

An engineer, an experimental physicist, a theoretical physicist and a philosopher went for a walk in the Scottish Highlands. In a field in the distance, they saw a black sheep. "Look at that," said the engineer. "The sheep in Scotland are black."

"Well," said the experimental physicist. "Some of the sheep in Scotland are black."

"I think you mean," said the theoretical physicist, "that at least one of the sheep in Scotland is black."

"On one side, anyway," added the philosopher.

164 **Fuzzy logic**
The French philosopher Rousseau said: "Take the course opposite to custom and you will almost always do well." But how does this apply to bicycles with square wheels?

165 The light of wisdom

"How many philosophers does it take to change a light bulb?"

"Two: one to argue that it is not dark, the other to argue that true light is impossible."

166 Borrower's bargain

A man borrowed some money from a friend to get out of a crisis. "Thank you very much for lending me this money," he said, "I'll be eternally in your debt."

"That's what I'm afraid of," replied his friend.

167 Think of others

It's OK to be you, to be who you really are. It's absolutely not OK to be somebody else. So spare a thought for people who are not you, who *are* somebody else.

168 Look both ways

"All saints have a past and all sinners have a future."

ANTON CHEKHOV (1860–1904)

169 Wrong moments

Our best thoughts usually come to us in situations where it is impossible either to write them down or to impress someone by speaking them aloud.

170 Transform the negative

Channel your fears into something more positive. Remember, Walt Disney was scared of mice.

171 From The Devil's Dictionary

"Acquaintance: A person whom we know well enough to borrow from but not well enough to lend to."

AMBROSE BIERCE (1842–1914)

172   Creative path

"Genius points the way, talent takes it."

MARIA VON EBNER-ESCHENBACH (1830–1916)

173   False security

If you can stay calm while all around you is chaos,
then you probably haven't understood the seriousness
of the situation.

174 **Winged messenger**
Love is like a butterfly. If you chase it, it will elude you. But if you just let it fly, it will come to you when you least expect it.

175 Progress
By the time you're about 50 years old, you imagine you've learned just about everything there is to know about life – but that's the time when everyone starts talking about machines you've never seen and music you've never heard.

176 Following through

Veni, Vidi, Velcro – I came, I saw and I stuck at it.

177 Simple precaution

Before you say something off the cuff, make sure your shirt is clean.

178 **Best efforts**
Do whatever you can to keep a smile on your face. If you can't lift the corners, let the middle sag.

179 Animal instincts
Don't believe that humans are the most intelligent species. Look at dolphins – it only takes them about a week to train someone to stand at the side of the pool and throw fish at them.

180 The chancer
"I get enough exercise pushing my luck."

181 A true friend

Your fridge likes you: that's why it puts the light on for you every time you open the door.

182 Be good!

How do you get rid of a bad habit? Just imagine that every time you indulge in it you're clocking up a month of community service in the roughest neighbourhood of heaven – which is just like the roughest neighbourhood of your own home town, except that there are no policemen.

183 A memorable gesture

Flatter someone and they may not believe you. Criticize someone and they probably won't like you. Ignore someone and they may never forgive you. But encourage someone and they'll never forget you.

184 Harsh criticism

"A drama critic is a man who leaves no turn unstoned."
GEORGE BERNARD SHAW (1856–1950)

185 Mischief rules

Finding the inner child can be difficult for some
people. They imagine you have to recapture the
innocence of childhood. You don't. All you have to
do is chalk "FOOL" on the back of someone's coat and
wait for the fun to start.

186 Animal crackers

Well OK, so elephants and buzzards mate for life. So
do swans. But is it really that big a deal? After all, if
you're a buzzard you're probably not going to find a
buzzard that's any better-looking than the one you've
got, so why not mate for life?

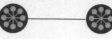

187 **Celebrate!**
Birthdays are good for you. Research has shown that the more you have, the longer you live.

188 **Persian proverb**
Squeeze the past like a sponge, smell the present like a rose, and send a kiss to the future.

189 **Cheers!**
A man walks into a bar with a lump of asphalt under his arm. "What'll it be?" asks the barman. "A whisky and soda," says the man, "and one for the road."

190   Arab proverb

He who knows not, and knows not he knows not – he is a fool. Shun him.

He who knows not, and knows he knows not – he is simple. Teach him.

He who knows and knows not he knows – he is asleep. Waken him.

He who knows and knows he knows – he is wise. Follow him.

191   Mutual muddle

"How do you confuse a frog?"

"Put it in a round bowl and tell it to take a nap in the corner."

"How does a frog confuse you?"

"By coming out and saying he needed that nap and feels much better now."

192   Backward thinking

What would a chair look like if your
knees bent the other way?

193   Zen saying

When an ordinary man attains knowledge, he is a
sage; when a sage attains understanding, he is an
ordinary man.

194   Breakdown cover

A smile is the lighting system of the face, the cooling
system of the head and the heating system of the
heart. A frown is a flat tyre. A hug from someone you
love is free roadside assistance.

195   Small people

To belittle is to be little.

196   Bar joke

A horse walks into a bar. The barman says, "Why the long face?"

197   When less is more

In life, it is better to understand a little than to misunderstand a lot.

198   Modern art

All styles of art reflect their times, even still-life and portraiture. Painters of still-lifes are now painting their fruit without a blemish and wrapped in a see-through vacuum pack.

199   Cover up

If at first you don't succeed, destroy all the evidence that you tried.

200   The march of time

You know you're getting older when you bend to tie your shoelaces and wonder what else you can do while you're down there.

201   Natural break

A conclusion is the place you reach when you get tired of thinking.

202   Reality check

We're not supposed to be perfect. If we were, they wouldn't make pencils with erasers.

203   On the level

Once the game is over, the king and the pawn go back into the same box.

ITALIAN PROVERB

204 Out with it

Don't bottle up your feelings. A restless dog in a small room is mad; but let him loose in the park and he's just playful.

205 Nature's way

Wear white, natural fabrics – they'll help to induce a feeling of calm and purity. Sheep swear by them.

206 Vanishing trick

My husband seems not to care about his appearance. He hasn't made one for three weeks now.

207 High ambition

"What do you want to be when you grow up?" a little girl was asked by one of her mother's friends. "An archangel's personal assistant," she replied.

208 Why say not yes?

The word NO has two letters in it. The word YES contains three letters. That's 50 percent extra, just for changing your mind.

209 Every coin has two sides

Just because a person is a vegetarian, it might not mean they love animals – they might just hate plants.

210 Straight to the top

"Enthusiasm is the great hill-climber."

ELBERT HUBBARD (1856–1915)

211 Against the odds

A university degree is something to proud of. It shows that one has succeeded in gaining recognition for academic excellence despite the distractions pursued and the teaching endured.

212 Wealth warning

It's not enough to live within your earnings. You have to live within your yearnings as well.

213 **Only appearances**

Going to church doesn't make you a good person any more than standing in a garage makes you a Cadillac.

214 **Perspectives**

A pessimist is someone who sees today as the yesterday they will worry about tomorrow, and panics. An optimist is someone who realizes today is the tomorrow they worried about yesterday, and smiles.

215 **What really matters**

Remember: quality not quantity. A dung beetle lays more eggs than an organic hen.

216 **Digging the dirt**

"What is the definition of an archaeologist?"
"A person whose career is in ruins."

217   In the groove

Life is like a children's playground. It don't mean a thing if it ain't got that swing.

218   Quiet please!

For a long life, breathe through your nose. For a long and happy life, shut your mouth while you're doing it.

219   Brain and brawn

"What do you call a big, strong guy who loves books?"

"Conan the Librarian."

220   Artistic struggle

"Painting is not very difficult when you don't know how; but when you do know how – ah, then it's a different matter."

EDGAR DEGAS (1834–1917)

221 **Warm welcome**

The gentle art of hospitality is to make your guests feel at home, even when you wish they were.

222 **Just an idea**

Could you even begin to imagine a world with no hypothetical situations?

223 **Techno-blip**

To err is human, but to really foul things up requires a computer.

224 **Get out more!**

How long has it been since you painted the town red? Is it time for a second coat?

225   Chinese proverb

People who say it cannot be done are often
interrupted by the person doing it.

226   Spick and span

Carry a feather duster with you wherever you go. It
will bring only happiness – if you can't find someone
to tickle, at least you'll be able
to do their dusting.

227 Not a sound

A woman gave her granddaughter a conch shell, saying if she listened carefully she would hear the sea. The girl put it to her ear for a few moments, then turned to her gran and said, "I think the tide must be out!"

228 Travelling light

Abandoning your faith because it fails to satisfy the requirements of reason is like taking the batteries out of your flashlight to make it lighter to carry.

229 Empty calories

Eating popcorn is about as nutritious as licking postage stamps.

230 Double dealing

A businessman wanted to give a politician a sports car.

"I'm afraid," said the politician, "that my basic sense of ethics, decency and fair play means that I could not possibly accept this gift."

"How about I sell it to you for the price of a cup of coffee?" said the businessman. The politician thought for a while. "I'll take two," he replied.

231   Great expectations

"Duty is what one expects from others, it is not what one does oneself."

OSCAR WILDE (1854–1900)

232   Proverbial wisdom

"It is better to be silent and be thought a fool than to speak out and remove all doubt."

SOMETIMES ATTRIBUTED TO ABRAHAM LINCOLN (1809–1865)

233   Tall order

The American humorist Robert Benchley reported that once he came out of a night club and, seeing a uniformed figure, tapped him on the shoulder and said, "Get me a cab." The man swung round in a fury and asserted that he was not a porter, he was a rear admiral. "OK," said Benchley, "get me a battleship."

234 Positive spin

Most people are pessimists. When things go bump in the night, how many of us think it might be an undercover philanthropist on a secret mission to redistribute his wealth?

235 **Absolute zero**
If it's zero degrees outside today and it's supposed to be twice as cold tomorrow, how cold is it going to be?

236 **No-horse town**
"The most striking thing about the city of Venice is the complete absence of the smell of horse dung."

ALPHONSE ALLAIS (1854–1905)

237 **Predator sport**
When the owl goes to the mice's picnic, he isn't there to admire the sack races.

238 Helping hands
Don't just stand there
with your hands in
your pockets.
Put them to work –
give someone a hug.

239 Where the heart is
"The home is not the tame place in the world of
adventure. It is the one wild place in the world
of rules and set tasks."

G.K. CHESTERTON (1874–1936)

240   **Dead language**

Latin, like the mysterious statues on Easter Island, was largely invented to baffle posterity.

241   Soul music

Happiness can't be learned, and it can't be forced.
The feet may learn the steps, but only the soul can
truly dance.

242   Lucky Peter

During a grammar class, the teacher spots one of her
pupils staring out the window. "Hey, Peter!" she shouts,
"Give me two pronouns." Peter answers, "Who? Me?"

243   Overheard at a party

"My dear Felicity, I haven't seen you for ages!"
"I thought I told you to wait in the car."

244   Say thank you

He who is carried on another's back does not
appreciate how far the town is.
AFRICAN PROVERB

245   Happy holidays

First man: "I'm free to do whatever I like at the moment. My wife's gone for a two-month vacation in the Caribbean."

Second man: "Jamaica?"

First man: "No, it was her own idea."

ADAPTED FROM A CARTOON IN *PUNCH*, 1914

246   Full of energy

Chinese medicine is based on the principle that the body is charged with life energy, called chi. That's why chihuahuas bark so much.

247   Modest proposal

"I had rather men should ask why no statue has been erected in my honour, than why one has."

MARCUS PORCIUS CATO (234–149BC)

248 **Little green men**

Martians have already invaded our planet. They beat us to the only available parking spaces in town, make the TV go haywire, and brainwash our husbands to forget important anniversaries.

249 **Tower of tales**

"What building has the most stories?"

"The library."

250 **Laugh-free zone**

Many directors of comic movies today are obviously inspired by the silent movies of the past – when they show something intended to be funny, the audience don't make a sound.

251 **Which way?**

If all roads lead to Rome, how do you get to Minnetonka?

252 **No limit**

"Genius may have its limitations, but stupidity is not thus handicapped."

ELBERT HUBBARD (1856–1915)

253   Off the cuff

"If I am to speak for ten minutes, I need a week for preparation; if fifteen minutes, three days; if half an hour, two days; if an hour, I am ready now."

WOODROW WILSON (1856–1924)

254   Riding the wave

Just as surfers can wait a lifetime for the Great Wave, so liars occasionally get their moment of glory, when seven or eight lies suddenly coincide into one Great Whopper.

255   Faking it

Some people go to elaborate lengths in order to massage a loved one's ego. An example would be those women who make their family move to the San Andreas fault so that one day they may be able to persuade their husbands that the earth moved.

256 Let it rain

One great advantage of being a gardener is the double satisfaction you get when it rains – the garden gets a lovely refreshing drink, and you have a good excuse to stay inside with a lovely refreshing drink.

257 Grumble chart

The graph a doctor checks at the end of a hospital bed registers how much a patient has grumbled since the last visit.

258 **Practicalities**

One Saturday afternoon a man walked into a grocery store and said, "I want to buy all the rotten eggs you have."

"Certainly," said the grocer. "Do you want them to throw at the new mayor who's going to make a speech in the town square tomorrow morning?"

"I *am* the new mayor," said the man.

259   Famous

"My address? I think 'Italy' will be sufficient."

GIUSEPPE VERDI (1813–1901)

260   A celebration

A couple were celebrating their wedding anniversary. As a surprise, their children cooked them a fabulous meal, laid the table beautifully, and then went out leaving a note saying, "Spoil yourselves! Do something we wouldn't do."

The husband looked at the wife and shrugged. "Well, I suppose we could vacuum the living room."

261   Mad about games

Children who spend all day playing computer games become over-competitive. As a parent you'll notice this when they start racing each other to drive you mad.

262   Roof raids

In the old days it was common for burglars to strip the lead off church roofs. Pencils were rare and very expensive then.

263   Fashion statement

Body jewelry is an increasingly popular way to rebel against society, but a less painful way would be to wear tweeds inside out.

264   Keeping busy

"A great success! I had two secretaries, one to answer my letters, the other to send locks of hair to my admirers. I have had to let them both go, poor fellows: one is in hospital with writer's cramp, and the other is quite bald."

OSCAR WILDE (1854–1900), COMMENTING ON A U.S. LECTURE TOUR

265 The shock of his life

A man fainted and was revived by paramedics. When asked what happened he replied, "My son asked me for the keys to the garage, and instead of coming out with the car he came out with the lawnmower!"

266 Enjoy!

You can indeed have too much of a good thing – and sometimes it's fabulous.

267   Returning the compliment

The authorities of the city of Paris have had a beach installed alongside the River Seine for the recreation of locals and visitors, about a mile from Notre Dame. Inspired by this, the authorities of Bondi Beach in Australia are planning to install a huge Gothic cathedral on an island about half a mile offshore.

268   How would I know?

A famous TV star was recognized by someone in the street. "Didn't I see you on television last night?" asked the passer-by.

"I'm sorry, I don't know," replied the star. "When I'm on TV, I can't see out!"

269   On time

Punctuality is something that, if you have it, all too often there's nobody around to share it with you.

270 Reassurance

"Doris, the audience are not actually hissing you; it's just a lot of people whispering to each other, 'That's Doris Cooper, Gladys Cooper's sister.'"

NOEL COWARD (1899–1973)

271 Learning by example

Everyone learns from other people's mistakes – none of us have time to think them all up for ourselves.

272 Dress sense

"I always wear battledress. It is practical, simple, cheap and does not go out of fashion."

FIDEL CASTRO (b.1926)

273 **Sorry, I missed that?**

Certain sounds in nature are beyond the range of human hearing – like the "thank you" spoken by an immigration officer at passport control.

274 **Sad story**

"When decorating I always use a step-ladder. I don't really get on with my real ladder."

HARRY HILL (b.1964)

275 **In the farmyard**

"What has four legs and goes 'Boo'?"
"A cow with a head-cold."

276 **The art of recall**

Everyone has a photographic memory – it's just that some of us have run out of film.

277 Sweet nothings

Not all decisions are best made by adults. For example, allow your inner child to choose your breakfast cereal. She will select it for the free toy, not the nutritional value: it will taste ten times better, and it will put a smile on your face.

278 Message from above

"My theory, briefly, is that the universe was dictated but not signed."

CHRISTOPHER MORLEY (1890–1957)

279 Disguises

We all make mistakes, and we all have our own ways of covering them up. Builders cover theirs with ivy and chefs cover theirs with mayonnaise. Cover your mistake with a smile, and no one will know you ever made it.

280   Questions and answers

If you ask a silly question, you'll get a silly answer.
Ask a silly person, you'll get an even sillier answer.
And don't even think about asking a silly person a
silly question.

281 # Is it worth it?
Living on Earth is expensive, but it does include a trip around the Sun every year.

282 **Chinese proverb**
A bird does not sing because it has an answer. It sings because it has a song.

283 **Local ad**
Wanted: fall guy for famous comedian. To sweep up leaves in garden of New England mansion.

284   For better or worse

A woman marries a man expecting he will change,
but he doesn't. A man marries a woman expecting
she won't change, but she does.

285   Root race

Time is just the clever device that nature uses to
inconvenience people who dye their hair.

286   Loose morals

"I would suggest the following rider to the Ten
Commandments: candidates should not
attempt more than six of these."

HILAIRE BELLOC (1870–1953)

287   Stay in the moment

Don't let the past hold you back – you're missing the
good stuff.

288 Action point

Don't sit there wishing that somebody would come along with a shovel to enlarge the rock pool and make it deep enough to swim in – just turn around and walk to the ocean.

289 Back to nature

Discover wildlife! Have kids!

290 Fast motion

Watching old silent movies can tell you a lot about our yesteryears – including how much faster the pace of life was in those days.

291 Real manners

Just because you *can* do something, it doesn't mean that you *should*. A true gentleman is someone who can play the bagpipes, but doesn't.

292   **Psychology lesson**

A boy went to the doctor's to have an injection. When it was all over, the doctor went to put a bandage on the affected area, but the boy asked for it to be put on the other arm. "But I want your friends to know that you've had an injection and to be careful of your arm," said the doctor.

The boy gave him a withering look. "You don't know much about kids, do you, Doc?" he replied.

293   **Mystery malady**

A wife is visiting her husband in hospital.

Husband: "I'm worried, dear, I don't think the doctors know what's wrong with me"

Wife: "What makes you say that?"

Husband: "The suggestions box at the end of the bed."

294   **Chinese proverb**

A smile will earn you ten more years of life.

295   **Amateur spirit**

Don't be put off anything by a lack of expertise. Remember, the ark was built by amateurs; the *Titanic*, by professionals.

296   **Poor me!**

Did you hear about the paranoid with low self-esteem? He thought nobody important was out to get him.

297 Where are we? Cellphones serve a useful social purpose in reminding forgetful passengers that they are on a train or bus.

298 Sabotage

Anyone can say the right thing at the right time. The real skill comes in not saying the wrong thing at the perfect moment.

299 Hush money

A little boy became restless during a sermon. He turned to his mother. "Mom," he whispered, "if we give him the money now, will he let us go?"

300 Master chef

"Can your husband cook?"
"Let's just say that he tends to burn the salad."

301 It's only common sense

Laugh and the world laughs with you. Cry and you have to blow your nose.

302   Two kinds of people

"Some cause happiness wherever they go; others whenever they go."

OSCAR WILDE (1854–1900)

303   Sweet and sour

Tomatoes grow sweeter with age; a bottle of milk goes sour. Live your life like a tomato, and don't cry over spilt milk.

304   Brotherly love

Little Jimmy was becoming jealous of his new brother. When he overheard his parents saying they would have to move because the place wasn't big enough for the four of them, he told them ruefully, "I wouldn't bother. He's already learned how to crawl – he'd only follow us ..."

305   **Progress report**
I have every intention
of living forever.
So far I'm not doing
too badly.

306   **Ships in the night**
"Geniuses are like
ocean liners: they
should never meet."
LOUIS ARAGON (1897–1982)

307   **All smiles**
What does it matter if
it's raining? Declare
your umbrella a
frown-free zone.

308 Monkey business

Never try to teach a gorilla
to play the clarinet.
It's a complete waste of
your time, and it will really
annoy the gorilla, who is
much more suited to
playing a stringed
instrument.

309 Mud mask

A boy who had been playing football at school that afternoon came home with mud splashes all over him and said to his mom, "Who am I?"

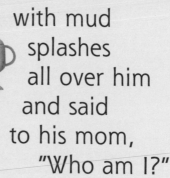

Happy to play along with the game, she replied, "I don't know! Who are you?"

"Wow!" exclaimed the boy. "Mrs Bateson was right! She said I was so dirty, my own mother wouldn't recognize me!"

310 **Much more likely**

A little girl was telling her mom how Moses crossed the Red Sea.

"First he assembled a team of the world's best engineers, then he built an enormous bridge that went all the way across."

"Are you sure that's what you've been taught?" asked her mother. The little girl looked a bit sheepish.

"To be honest, Mom, if I told you what we've been taught you'd never believe it."

311 **Unlucky charm**

It's terribly bad luck to be superstitious.

312 **Family and friends**

Imagine your life is a film. It doesn't really matter if you don't understand the plot, so long as you have a brilliant cast.

313   Honest at least
Teacher: "You haven't listened to a word I've said. Are you having trouble hearing?"
Pupil: "No, miss. I'm having trouble listening."

314   Self-evident
There have always been times like these.

315   Romantics beware
Don't marry a tennis player: love is nothing to them.

316   Next time
A young couple brought their new baby home. After a few days, the wife suggested that her husband change the diaper. "I'll do the next one," he said. When the time came for the diaper to be changed again, she called her husband. "I didn't mean the next diaper," he replied. "I meant the next baby."

317 **Split personality**
Sometimes the inner child
disgraces itself – and all we can
do is watch from a distance,
shaking our heads in disapproval.

318 **Stressbusters**
Smiles may not pay the rent ... but they save you the
cost of therapy!

319 **Real mix-up**
Others first put.

320 Christmas is coming

A few scientific experts on climate are now arguing that forecasts of global warming are flawed because there's a compensatory effect they don't take into account – the gradual expansion of Christmas.

321 Stay-at-home

A teenage boy with nose-rings and purple hair was overheard saying to one of his friends, "I don't really like to go around looking like this, but it stops my parents from dragging me everywhere with them."

322 African proverb

When you are in love, a cliff becomes a meadow.

323 Brainstorm

Memory is the key, but I'm sorry, I can't remember where the lock is!

324   Role reversal

It's very therapeutic to talk about your problems. If you've had a bad day, phone a friend. You'll get things off your chest, and soon you'll find you're not even talking about your problems any more – you're talking about theirs!

325   Walk don't run

St Augustine said, "Solvitur ambulando" – solve it by walking. But he didn't have skiing injuries in mind, nor your car breaking down a hundred miles from Las Vegas.

326   Topsy turvy

"To make a wish, you throw a coin into a wishing well. Or if you haven't got a wishing well, you can stand on your head and throw a coin down the chimney."
MATTHEW, AGED 8

327   Rousing the rebels

You have nothing to lose but your shoelaces – workers of the world, untie!

328   Green fingers

Everyone you meet has a flower in their heart.
Water it with your smile.

329   Wild West

"What happened to the cowboy who dressed up in newspaper?"
"He was arrested for rustling."

330   Hard of hearing

Aspiring artist: "OK, I've bought two dozen cows, some milking equipment and a three-legged stool."
Mentor: "You fool, I said you should keep a diary, not a dairy!"

331   Major blunder

"The greatest mistake you can make in life is to be continually fearing you will make one."

ELBERT HUBBARD (1856–1915)

332   Poetic yearnings

Oh for the wings of a dove! Or, failing that, a juicy chicken leg would do nicely.

333   Empty-handed

"I smiled at my daddy, and he smiled back and gave me some pocket money. So I tried walking into the bank and smiling there but my head was below the level of the cashier's counter, so I didn't get anything."

JENNIFER, AGED 9

334   Never delay

Do it today: tomorrow it might be illegal.

335   Help is at hand

When a person suffers from low self-esteem, friends may find it difficult to provide constructive help. You try little morale-boosting gestures and carefully judged assurances. But next time, why don't you just go ahead and say what you think: "You must be a great person or you wouldn't have a friend like me."

336 **In reverse**

If you got into a taxi and he started driving backwards, would the taxi driver end up owing you money?

337   Real pal

A true friend is not the person who buys you an expensive lunch, but the one who tells you quietly that you have a piece of cabbage stuck in your teeth.

338   The botanist speaks

Johnny was learning about trees in Biology, and how you can tell their age from their rings. At breakfast one morning, he was offered a cinnamon Danish. "I can't eat that!" he exclaimed, "It's five years old!"

339   Pure giving

The enlightened person shows hospitality to strangers for their sake – and not just because one of them may be a rich, long-lost relative in disguise, secretly checking that there isn't anyone in the family who needs a dollar or two.

340 Magic moment

You must be clear about your goals and move toward them with resolve, one step at a time. You could try saying "Abracadabra", but that only tends to work when there's a z in the name of the month.

341 Eastern know-how

I got bored with *feng shui* and so I redesigned my house on the principles of *chow mein*: all wiggly and jumbled up.

342 Bloodline

"Insanity is hereditary: you get it from your children."
SAM LEVENSON (1911–1980)

343 Toddler trouble

Never ask a two-year-old to hold a tomato.

344 **Two-timer**

A person with a watch knows what time it is. A person with two watches is never quite sure.

345 Mood of the gods

"A rainbow is the bunting they put up in Heaven to celebrate the end of a storm."

FIONA, AGED 10

346 Everything's possible

"If" – a harmless word, but one that is banned from your dreams.

347 Kitchen lore

You can never have too many mugs.

348 Opposites

A dancer goes quick on her beautiful legs; a duck goes quack on her beautiful eggs.

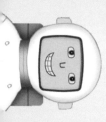

349 **Seafood surprise**
The world's your clam.
(Oysters are so last year!)

350 **Proverbial wisdom**
A miss is as good as a mister.

351 **Aim for the skies**
I bought a space heater the other day. If it can't keep me warm on a camping trip in New Hampshire, I don't know how it's going to help me out on Pluto.

352 **Milky way**
If you told a cow a really funny joke, could she laugh so much that milk would come out of her nose?

353 **Sweet and wicked**
Forbidden fruit creates many jams.

354   Wishing well

A good friend will find the joy in your life like a
dowser finding water in the desert.

355   Starting young

All toddlers can benefit from nursery school. It's never
too early to start laying the foundations of a good
résumé.

356   Everyday medicine

"I'd like to see the doctor, please?"

"Which doctor?"

"No, just an ordinary one."

TAIDG, AGED 10

357   Off the cuff

Improvising is a great adventure – a class act needs no
cue cards.

358 **Tails you win**

Money can buy you a great dog, but it won't buy a wag of its tail.

359 **A real buzz**

Beekeeping is a fine and productive hobby for anyone who lives in the country. Town-dwellers can also enjoy this activity if they dress their kids in striped sweaters and get them to run around flapping their arms and making buzzing noises.

360 **Simplify your life**

Bringing order to the world's confusions can start with tidying one over-cluttered closet.

361 **Mr Perfect**

I married Mr Right. But I didn't know then that his first name was Always

362   What a picture

Show yourself in your true colours: pink, black or brown with a splash of brown, black, yellow or gray on top, and with a pair of little green, brown, gray or blue dots just underneath.

363   Lazy days

"Summer afternoon – summer afternoon ... the two most beautiful words in the English language."

HENRY JAMES (1843–1916)

364   Drama in court

A defendant in a court case stood up in the dock and said to the judge before the trial started, "I don't recognize this court!"

"Why not?" asked the judge.

"You must have had it decorated since the last time I was here."

Tale of a toothbrush

365

One night before bed
Harry, a three-year-old,
proudly told his
grandmother that he'd
brushed not only his own
teeth but also the dog's.
The next day his
grandmother bought
Harry a new toothbrush.
"Why did you buy me this?"

he asked.
"Because you
brushed the
dog's teeth
with your old
one, Harry."
"No I didn't,
Gran," he said.
"I used yours."

366   Buenas noches!

The Spanish are renowned for the late hours they keep.
Spain is the only country in the world where you can
call a friend at midnight and say, "What shall we do
tonight?"

367   Engine trouble

"Dad, I've just been out in the car. It isn't running too
well. There's water in the carburettor."
"Where *is* the car, son?"
"In the lake."

368   Down on the farm

A kid on vacation from the city is staying on a farm
with his family. "No wonder Mama Pig is so huge," he
says to his brother after taking a walk on his own
around the farmyard. "There's a bunch of little pigs out
there blowing her up like a balloon!"

369 Get rich quick

Write down your current salary and add a couple of zeros at the end of it. Such a small thing, and all it would cost your employer is $00. Rehearse this argument, pluck up the courage, and go for it!

370 Notice on a fax machine

Operators with long hair are advised to wear a hair-net when using this fax. Otherwise they might find themselves in Hong Kong.

371 Feminine wiles

The best way to get a man to do something is to suggest that he's too old for it.

372 Tongue-tied

I'm not normally one to mince words, but th isti mel ha vel ittl eopt ion.

373 All about kids

"Before I was married, I had a hundred theories about raising children and no children. Now, I have three children and no theories."

JOHN WILMOT (1647–1680)

374 Animal ambition

A dog applied for a job with the foreign service and passed all the exams easily.
"You'll also need to show you're bilingual," said the interviewer.
"Miaow!" said the dog.

375 Proverbial wisdom

"No, thank you" has lost many a good butter-cake.

376 History lesson

Teacher: "In 1940, what were the Poles doing
in Russia?"
Pupil: "Holding up the telephone lines?"

377 Music lesson

"What do you get when you drop a piano down a
mine shaft?"
"A flat minor."

378 Old bones

"In a museum in Havana there are two skulls of
Christopher Columbus – one when he was a boy and
one when he was a man."

MARK TWAIN (1835–1910)

379 Marriage mishap

A marriage ceremony was taking place in the Leaning Tower of Pisa. The bride was just arriving at the foot of the tower when her intended fell off the balcony at the summit and landed on her. This naturally cast a groom over the entire proceedings.

380 Overdressed

0 and 8 are talking a walk in the desert. The 0 turns to the 8 and says, "You must be hot with that belt on."

THEO, AGED 8

381 Good companion

"The great pleasure of a dog is that you make a fool of yourself with him and not only will he not scold you, he will make a fool of himself too."

SAMUEL BUTLER (1835–1902)

382 **Guest pests**

A good way to deal with guests who've outstayed their welcome is to ask them if they'll help you prepare with your evening ritual: setting the rat traps.

383 **Safe and sound**

Quick-Air is one of the safest airlines in the world. All the pilots are trained in deep-sea rescue work.

384 **How to live**

You come into the world crying while all around you are smiling. Live your life so that you leave it smiling while all around you are crying.

385 **Ocean legend**

Last night I went to a concert by the Bermuda Symphony Orchestra. They played the coconuts beautifully but the triangle kept disappearing.

386 Life's imperfections

We live in an imperfect world. There are too many traffic wardens and the stone's too big in an avocado.

387 African proverb

If a naked man runs through your village in the middle of the night, be sure to get dressed before you chase him.

388 Economics forever

The age of humankind is a wink in the eye of eternity – a sobering thought if you've just shelled out the cash to take a teenager through college.

389 Outside chance

The odds against becoming a millionnaire before you're twenty are about the same as the odds against a goldfish's shoelaces coming undone.

Perspective is everything

A man goes round to his friend's house, and finds him playing chess with his pet dog.

"That," says the man, "is the most amazing dog I've ever seen!"

"Oh, I don't know about that," says the friend.

"I've beaten him four games out of five."

391 Time was

A cultural renaissance is returning this country to its golden age – when mammoths and dinosaurs roamed the icy wastes.

392 Hard sell

He's such a good salesman, he could sell a beach vacation to a Hawaiian.

393 Streetwise

City shopping streets are so crowded these days that walking along them's a serious challenge – like skiing up a rocky hillside.

394 **Christmas cracker**
"What do you call Santa's assistants?"
"Subordinate clauses."

395 **Gales of laughter**
Life is a beautiful flag, and laughter is the wind that makes it wave.

396 **Wake-up call**
The most lovely sound in the world is that of an alarm clock – announcing a new act in life's great adventure.

397 **On top of it all**
So long as you can laugh, you're still winning.

398   Game or blame

Stay in touch with your inner child: fingerpaint more, fingerpoint less.

399   Magic touch

If you have touched one person today with love and joy, then already your day has been rich.

400   Flip side

Dreams reveal the side of ourselves that we've omitted from our résumé.

401   You are what you eat

An optimist is someone who thinks eating equal amounts of carbohydrate and protein adds up to a balanced diet. A delusionist is someone who thinks the same about dark chocolate and white chocolate.

402   Life's rhythms

Sleep is the time when our nerves get soothed by the body's invisible healing mechanisms – prior to the kids jangling them up again next morning.

403   Justifiably cross

The reason swans look so angry is that people will insist on walking too close to their lake.

404   When darkness falls

Love is a game that's never called off because of poor light.

405   Even balance

Customer in a grocery store:
"One pound of mixed nuts please – and go easy on the coconuts."

406   Sweet affection

"I call my mom Yummy because she
smells like candy."

JANE, AGED 5

407 Lost in the mall

A little boy lost contact with his mother in a
shopping mall. So he went up to a
policeman and said, "Please could you help
me find a lady who's here without a little boy
who looks like me?"

408   The first couple

Adam and Eve had a perfect marriage. Adam didn't
have to listen to Eve saying that other men could have
done it better, and Eve didn't have to listen to Adam
saying he'd do it after his night out with the boys.

409 Man and beast

"Hey, is the bull in this field safe?" shouted the rambler to the farmer who was working in his farmyard on the other side of the fence.

"Well, put it this way," replied the farmer, "he's a whole lot safer than you are."

410 **Good point**

Why do ballet dancers always dance on their toes?
Wouldn't it be easier to just hire taller dancers?

411 **Getting to know you**

"You can discover more about a person in an hour of play than in a year of conversation."

PLATO (427–347BC)

412 **Schedules**

You don't have to work hard by burning the midnight oil. You can also do it by burning the midday oil.

413   Facts of life

Your children have started growing up when they stop asking you where they came from and start refusing to tell you where they're going.

414   Fine distinction

Knowledge and wisdom are not the same thing. Knowledge is knowing that a tomato is a fruit, not a vegetable. Wisdom is knowing that you shouldn't include it in a fruit salad.

415   Time to act

Today is the day I must finally be decisive. At least, I think so.

416   Up and down

Be bold in what you stand for; and careful in what you fall for.

417   Age gracefully

You don't get old, you just become a classic.

418   Language logic

Have you noticed that people these days often say
"he was like" when they mean "he said"? How long
will it be before they are saying "raincoat" when they
mean "tablespoon"?

419   School shy

Mom: "Simon, eat your breakfast, it's time for school."

Simon: "I don't want to go to school."

Mom: "Why not?"

Simon: "Because all the children hate me."

Mom: "Nonsense! Now, eat up and get going."

Simon: "But .... why? Why do I have to?"

Mom: "Well, for one thing, it's Monday. And for
another thing ... you're the head teacher!"

420   **Give generously**
"All who would win joy,
must share it; happiness
was born a twin."
LORD BYRON (1788–1824)

421   **Water music**
A brook would lose its song
if God removed the rocks.

422   **Wheely exhausted**
A bicycle can't stand on its
own because it's two-tyred.

423   **Benevolence**
A candle loses nothing by
lighting another candle.

424 **Accept life's ups and downs**

The world won't treat you fairly because you're good, any more than a lion won't eat you because you're a vegetarian.

425 **From The Devil's Dictionary**

"Harangue: A speech by an opponent, who is known as an harang-outang."

AMBROSE BIERCE (1842–1914)

426   North and South

Abraham Lincoln was once talking with a woman about how the North must treat the South. She disagreed with him, and said that she felt that we must destroy our enemies. Lincoln replied, "What, madam? Do I not destroy them when I make them my friends?"

427   Two rules

Don't sweat the petty things and don't pet the sweaty things.

428   Serial abstinence

I've never had any problem with addictions. Giving up coffee, for example, gets easier every time I do it.

429   Fill up first

There's one basic principle of domestic economy: never visit the supermarket before you've eaten.

430   Sands of time

We all sometimes have the feeling that time is running out. The only person who got everything done by Friday was Robinson Crusoe.

431   Song of joy

"Dance like nobody's watching,
Love like you've never been hurt,
Sing like nobody's listening,
Live like it's heaven on earth."

MARK TWAIN (1835–1910)

432   A pinch of salt

A father was reading his son the story of Lot in the Bible. He explained that Lot was told to take his wife and flee from the city, but his wife looked back and turned into a pillar of salt. The little boy looked aghast. "What happened to the flea?" he asked.

433 Self-knowledge
What a fine thing
experience is!
It enables us to
recognize a
mistake every
time we make it.

434　Eternal beauty

A fair face may fade, but a beautiful soul lasts forever.

435　Old blessings

"Make new friends but keep the old.
One is silver, and the other is gold."

ANONYMOUS

436　A definition

Alarm clock: A small tabletop device used to wake up people who don't have children.

437　Tommy tadpole?

"I want to give my pet tadpole a name, but it's really hard. If give him a name that suits him now, how do I know it will still suit him when he puts on his frogman's suit?"

OLIVER, AGED 5

438   Rhyme and reason

All the king's horses and all the king's men? Are you kidding me? No wonder they couldn't put Humpty together again. Just what did they expect the horses to do, anyway?

439   Stages of youth

Children go through four life stages with their fathers. First, they call you da-da. Then they call you daddy. Next they call you dad. Finally they call you collect.

440   Baby wisdom

Babies have a lesson for us: a smile is possible even before you can hold your head high.

441   Live and let live

The fly on your ice cream may not be there to annoy you: it's probably just there for the skiing.

442 **A law of economics**

A budget is something we go without to stay within.

443 **Hybrid**

If you cross a four-leaf clover with poison ivy, would you get a rash of good luck?

444 **Scent of content**

Happiness is like perfume: if you spray it on someone else, it's bound to rub off on you.

445 **It could be worse**

If you've been fishing for several hours and haven't caught anything except an old rubber boot, remember: you're still better off than the worm.

446 **Esperanto**

Everybody smiles in the same language.

447 Table manners

A little boy was talking to a farmer. "What have you got in your truck?" he asked.

"Manure," replied the farmer.

"What are you going to do with it?"

"Put it on my potatoes," replied the farmer.

The little boy shrugged. "You should come and have dinner with us. We put butter and salt on ours."

448 Don't panic!

When you find yourself on the wrong train, there's little to be gained by running down the corridor at top speed in the opposite direction.

449 Universal prayer

May I have the serenity to accept the things I cannot change, the courage to change the things I can, and a big suitcase full of used banknotes.

450 **Spanish proverb**
How beautiful it is to do nothing, and then rest afterwards.

451   **Just maybe**

The holes in your Swiss cheese are somebody else's
Swiss cheese.

452   **Living in the moment**

Be happy with what you have. If you spend your life
looking for greener pastures, you might find you're
too old to climb the fence.

453   **Rounding down**

If God had intended us to use the metric system, there
would have been 10 disciples.

454   **Weather wise**

First pupil: "Great news! Teacher said we're going to
have a test today come rain or shine."
Second pupil : "Why is that good news?"
First pupil: "It's snowing!"

455   Life's ironies

The nature of life is such that if you tell your boss that you were late for work because your car broke down, the next day your car will break down.

456   Jamaican proverb

You no got smile on yo face, no use open shop.

457 **Game training**

Monopoly is a game that all children should be taught to play, as it teaches basic life skills – like patiently serving a prison sentence.

458 **A new discovery**

Scientists recently located the gene for military aptitude. They would have found it earlier but it was camouflaged.

459   **Chain of being**

Smiles are like yogurt: you need some to make more.

460   **Proverbial wisdom**

A hair in the head is worth two in the brush.

461   **Couplet**

"The love in your heart wasn't put there to stay.
Love isn't love till you give it away."

ANONYMOUS

462   **Asking for trouble**

Never ask a hairdresser whether you need a haircut.

463   **Middle way**

Don't believe everything you read. But don't disbelieve
everything you read either – policemen don't consider
it a very good excuse for breaking the speed limit.

464 **Catch those rays**

To love and be loved is like having the sun on your face and on your back at the same time.

465 **Grace**

A priest asked a little boy, "Do you pray before beginning your meals?"

"I don't have to," replied the little boy. "My mom's quite a good cook."

466 **Garden lore**

Happiness held is the seed; happiness shared is the flower.

467 **Practical advice**

Troubled person, on the phone: "Doctor, doctor, what can I do? My little boy has swallowed my pen!"
Doctor: "Use a pencil till I get there."

468 **Clumsy Claus**

Santa Claus wears a red suit because he loves a drop of red wine and the suit hides stains well. Why the white trim? Well, that's just vanity!

469 **Paper tiger**

Never argue with somebody who buys ink from a wholesaler.

470 **Obstacle course**

If you're being chased by a police dog, try not to go through a tunnel, then run on to a little seesaw, then jump through a hoop of fire. They're trained for that.

471 **Cannibal rights**

If a vegetarian eats vegetables, what does a humanitarian eat?

472 **Faint praise**

Teacher: "What's two plus three?"
Pupil: "Five."
Teacher: "Good."
Pupil: "Good? It's perfect!"

473 Household hint

Try and switch the light out for romantic reasons as often as you do it for economic reasons.

474 Danish proverb

The road to a friend's house is never too long.

475 Jungle wise

"What's big and gray, and mutters?"
"A mumbo jumbo."

476 Inner child

Stop playing at being so serious and start playing seriously.

477 Self-knowledge

Uncle Tom: "Eric, why are you scratching yourself?"
Eric: "Nobody else knows where I itch."

478 Crowd pleaser

There's a difference between self-esteem and self-importance. Self-esteem is taking part in the local marathon and knowing that you have a good chance of finishing the course. Self-importance is taking part in the marathon because a thousand spectators will be heartbroken if you don't.

479 He and she

What passes as a woman's intuition is usually nothing more than a man's transparency.

480 Talking bones

A skeleton walked into a bar and said, "I'll have a lager and a floormop please."

481 Bathtime jumble

"What's the difference between a Peeping Tom and someone who's just got out of the bath?"
"One's rude and nosy, and the other's nude and rosy."

482 A question of anatomy

"What flowers grow between your nose and chin?"
"Tulips."

483   In decline

Interviewed on Soviet TV in the 1960s, the USSR Agriculture Minister was asked how that year's harvest was doing. "Average. Worse than last year, but better than next!"

484 **Quick flash**

Watching lightning at night, a little girl said to her mother,
"Is that God taking pictures?"

485 You choose

"There are only two ways to live your life.
One is as though nothing is a miracle.
The other is as though everything is a miracle."

ALBERT EINSTEIN (1879–1955)

486 Built-in solution

The reverse of "stressed" is "desserts".

487   Now that you mention it ...

Sign on the back of a big, slow, expensive car:
"As a matter of fact, I DO own the road."

488   The magic of "mine"

There is only one pretty child in the world, and every
mother has it.

489   Two fruits

"Our earthly life's a thorny tree
on which grow two fruits sweet:
The blessed gift of poetry,
and joy when true friends meet."

SANSKRIT POEM

490   Uphill struggle

I keep trying to lose weight, but it keeps on finding
me again.

491　Top of the morning

"How do you greet a German barber?"

"Good morning, Herr Dresser."

492　True love

To love for the sake of being loved is human; to love for the sake of loving is angelic.

493　Payback time

If it's a man's world – let him clean it.

494　A language lesson

Sally, aged 10: "What does 'bicentenary' mean?"

Sally's mom: "It means something is two hundred years old. Often when we start a word with 'bi' it's related to the number two. Can you think of another word starting with 'bi'?"

Sally: "Buy one get one free?"

495 Welcome to the family!

A woman asked her friend's five-year-old son about his new baby brother, born the previous week. "I don't think he's very well," the boy answered. Knowing the family well and not having heard about any illness, the woman asked what the matter was. "I don't know," said the boy, "but he hasn't got out of bed yet."

496 **Barely possible**
Follow your dream – unless it's that one when you turn up at work without any clothes on.

497 **Scottish proverb**
You live a long time after you're laughed at.

498 **Are they content?**
"Before we set our hearts too much upon anything, let us first examine how happy those are who already possess it."

FRANÇOIS DE LA ROCHEFOUCAULD (1613–1680)

499 Mother love

"God could not be everywhere and therefore he made mothers."

JEWISH SAYING

500 Christmas carol

A four-year-old boy got home from school and told his mother that he'd learnt a new Christmas carol entitled "Dick the Horse". Puzzled, she asked him to sing it. He took a breath and began, "Dick the Horse with boughs of holly, fa la la la la…"

501 More than enough

Necessity may be the mother of invention, but superfluity is the father of fun.

502 Vertical take-off

Angels can fly because they take themselves lightly.

503   **Shifting sands**

Having made your sandcastle with love and skill, sit
proud and happy when the tide comes in.

504   **Character clue**

"You can tell a lot about a fellow's character by his way
of eating jellybeans."

RONALD REAGAN (1911–2004)

505   **Long memories**

Thousands of years ago, cats were worshipped as gods.
Cats have never forgotten this.

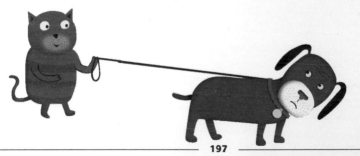

506 Freezing point

"Doctor, can you help me? My husband thinks he's a refrigerator. He sleeps with his mouth open, and the light keeps me awake."

507 Fine education

That best academy, a mother's knee.

508 Obstacle to freedom

A man noticed his neighbour's little son sitting alone on the sidewalk outside his house. He asked the boy what he was doing. "I've run away from home," came the reply. "You haven't got very far, have you?" said the man. The boy looked up and said, "I'm not allowed to cross the road on my own."

509 Life's a ball

It's not how far you fall, but how high you bounce.

510   Just desserts

The journalist Horatio Bottomley was sewing mail bags in prison (he had been jailed for fraud) when a visitor turned up to see him.

"Sewing, I see, Bottomley?" said the visitor.

"No, reaping," he replied.

511   Now is the season

"The time of the singing of birds is come."

THE SONG OF SOLOMON

512   Use both ears

People who speak more than they listen should consider how peculiar they would look if they had two mouths and one ear.

513   Sailor's wisdom

Smiles bridge oceans; frowns fill them with sharks.

514 Arc in the sky
At both ends
of the rainbow
there's a
wonderful world.

515 Not logical

"Happy as a dog with two tails," goes the popular
phrase – which is rather like saying "rich as a man
with two wallets."

516 Daily wonder

"To me every hour of the light and
dark is a miracle."

WALT WHITMAN (1819–1892)

517 Action!

Jesus is coming. Look busy!

518 By extension

If lawyers are disbarred and clergymen defrocked,
doesn't it follow that electricians can be delighted,
musicians denoted, cowboys deranged, models
deposed, and drycleaners depressed?

519 **Peace at last**

There never was a child so lovely but his mother was glad to get him asleep.

520 **Pet sounds**

Dogs come when they're called; cats take a message and get back to you later.

521 **Opting for joy**

Happiness is a choice we make every morning – a promise to ourselves, sworn on a waking smile.

522 **Consequences**

A teacher was telling one of her pupils not to pull faces. "When I was a little girl," she said, "I was told that if the wind changed my face would stick like that." "Well," replied the pupil, "you can't say you weren't warned."

523 One explanation

Elves are the burglars who've stolen something you need. Pixies are the policemen who've put it back in the wrong place.

524 Flight into Egypt

A Sunday School class was asked to draw a picture of any popular Bible story. Little Christopher drew four people on a plane, and the teacher asked him which story it was meant to represent. "The Flight into Egypt," said Christopher.

"I see," said the teacher. "So that must be Mary, Joseph, and Baby Jesus. But who's the fourth person?"

"Oh," said Christopher, "that's Pontius the Pilot."

525 Awakening world

A sign that spring's on its way: the first garden tools peeping above the snow.

526   Inheritance

Father: "Our son gets his exceptional brains from me, don't you think?"

Mother: "Probably. Mine were all still in place the last time I checked."

527   Sleep thief

The amount of sleep required by the average person is about a half-hour more.

528   Lovelorn

"Not only has Sebastian broken my heart and wrecked my life, he's also spoiled my entire evening!"

529   On vacation

"Nothing is really work unless you would rather be doing something else."

SIR JAMES M. BARRIE (1860–1937)

530 Jumbo geography

"In which countries are elephants found?"

"They're extremely large and intelligent and so never get lost."

531 Magic touch

A smile releases the genie from the bottle of routine.

532 Navigation aid

"Only the heart knows how to find what is precious."

FYODOR DOSTOYEVSKY (1821–1881)

533 **Good and bad**

"It's been my experience that folks who have no vices have very few virtues."

ABRAHAM LINCOLN (1809–1865)

534 **Marking time**

It's always dullest just before the yawn.

535 **Starting point**

A little girl was explaining to her friend what it means to be adopted. "It means," she explained, "that I grew in Mommy's heart, not in her tummy."

536 **Important sign**

Do not walk past the end of the pier.

537 **Fancy my tickle?**

Tickling is to humour as coughing is to singing.

538   Mr and Mrs Big

Appearances undersell us: we're bigger on the inside than on the outside.

539   Special offer

It's Happy Hour at the Chinese restaurant. For $5 you can have all the food you can eat with one chopstick.

540   Punctuality

"The best way I know to catch a train is to miss the one before."

ADAPTED FROM G.K. CHESTERTON (1874–1936)

541   Caught in the act

Gamekeeper: "Hey, you! Didn't you see that notice: 'Private: no fishing?'"
Poacher: "Sir, I could never be so rude as to read a private notice."

542   **Space landing**

"What do you do when you see a spaceman?"

"Park in it, man!"

543   **Him and me**

"We have a weird and wonderful relationship: he's weird and I'm wonderful."

544   **Drinking song**

One tequila, two tequila, three tequila, floor.

545   **Only believe**

Biting an apple is an act of faith. Start there and travel to the stars.

546   **Ride, don't drive**

A car may get you there sooner, but riding a horse will make you feel braver.

547 Poetic justice

"The liar's punishment is not that he is not believed, but that he cannot believe anyone else."

GEORGE BERNARD SHAW (1856–1950)

548 Best remedies

When you're feeling tired, sleep. When you're feeling stiff, exercise. When you're feeling sad, smile.

549 Abominable snowman

"What do you get when you cross a snowman with a vampire?"

"Frostbite."

550 Collector's item

"Dear Sir, I have a circular disk of black plastic, with concentric grooves all over its surface and a hole in the middle. Is this a record?"

551 A great invention
If it hadn't been for
Thomas Edison we'd all be
watching TV by candlelight.

552 Dear Peter
A mother overheard her
daughter's evening prayers,
which began: "Dear Peter,
please look after Mommy
and Daddy ..." She corrected
her, saying "Don't you mean
"Dear God'?"

"No," the little girl insisted,
"That's God's first name. At
the end of prayers at Sunday
School we always say,
"Thanks Peter God.'"

553 Fast living

"In skating over thin ice our safety is in our speed."

RALPH WALDO EMERSON (1803–1882)

554 Tough challenge

The exam questions were a cinch. It was the answers I had problems with!

555 Write it down

The palest ink is stronger than the clearest memory.

CHINESE PROVERB

556 Eminently practical

You can't have everything. Where would you put it?

557   Optional prayer

A little boy was saying his prayers. "Lord, help me to be a better person. But if you can't, don't worry – I'm having a pretty good time as it is!"

558   Light beams

"A good laugh is sunshine in a house."

WILLIAM MAKEPEACE THACKERAY (1811–1863)

559   Male advantage

It's great to be male: you can drop by and visit a friend without having to take them a little gift.

560   Dogs and cats

Animals are great levellers – they help you keep a true sense of proportion about your importance. So to achieve the right balance, you should have a dog that will worship you and a cat that will ignore you.

561 Strange encounter

A train traveller was puzzled by a fellow passenger who sat by the open window, muttering and tearing pages out of a book. Finally she asked him what he was doing.

"Keeping the wild elephants away," was the reply.

"But," said the woman, "there aren't any elephants around."

"No," said the man. "You see, it works!"

562 Sign on a New York freeway

All those in favor of conserving gasoline, please raise your right foot.

563 Happy naturalist

"It is perhaps a more fortunate destiny to have a taste for collecting shells than to be born a millionaire."

ROBERT LOUIS STEVENSON (1850–1894)

Young and old

A kindly old grandmother was testing her granddaughter on her times tables. The little girl got every question correct. After a while she looked at her grandmother in exasperation.

"Honestly, Granny," she said, "I really think you

should try and work some
of these out for
yourself."

565 Flood files

"Where did Noah keep his bees?"
"In archives!"

566 Moonlight serenade

"At the touch of love, everyone becomes a poet."

PLATO (427 – 347 BC)

567 Mind power

Age is an issue of mind over matter. If you don't mind,
it doesn't matter.

568 Everyday drama

If all the world's a stage, where is the audience sitting?

569 Keep still

The first rule of looking good: don't sneeze while
somebody is cutting your hair.

570　Still in business
It's not over till the fat lady sings. But just because you see a fat lady singing, it doesn't mean it's over.

571　Compensation
"To ease another's heartache is to forget one's own."
ABRAHAM LINCOLN (1809–1865)

572　Simple truth
The Law of Getting Things Done states that it always takes longer than you think to get things done, even when you take the Law of Getting Things Done into account.

573　Second best
If you can't catch a bird of paradise, be content with an old wet hen.
RUSSIAN PROVERB

574   The optimist

"I have not failed. I've just found 10,000 ways that won't work."

THOMAS EDISON (1847–1931)

575 **Horsing around**
"Let's play at being a horse, like they do in pantomimes. I'll be the front end. You can just be yourself."

576 **Springtime**
"One lovely smile can warm three winter months."
ADAPTED FROM A JAPANESE PROVERB

577   Wish control

Don't wish you weren't what you are now. You'll only find you wish you were what you were when you wished you weren't.

578   Trouble in space

"Hilarious, Scotty. Now could you please beam up my clothes?"

579   Proverbial wisdom

There's a helping hand at the end of your sleeve.

580   Precious little

"We ourselves feel that what we are doing is just a drop in the ocean, but the ocean would be less because of that missing drop."

MOTHER TERESA (1910–1997)

581   Mother's little helper

A little boy was allowed to feel the baby kick in the tummy of his pregnant mother. "How is the baby going to come out of there?" he asked, sounding concerned.

"Don't worry," said the mother, "the doctor will help."

The little boy's eyes widened even further. "You've got a doctor in there too?" he asked.

582   Breakfast

Consider the egg in the monastery – out of the frying pan and into the friar.

583   Child-free zone

Tense, nervous headache? Then do what it says on the bottle of painkiller pills – "Keep out of the reach of children."

584 **All-day party**
A good way to make a new friend is to smile at a stranger ... you'll be surprised how many people smile back.

585　Child's play

"You've been stuggling to finish your tax return all evening, and you're still not done. Why, a child of five could do better than that."

"Don't be silly, where am I going to find a child of five at this time of night?"

586　Just when you need it

Change is inevitable, except from a vending machine.

587　In the far north

First Eskimo: "Where did your mother come from?"

Second Eskimo: "Alaska."

First Eskimo: "Don't bother, I'll ask her myself."

588　Comic turn

"What do you call an unemployed jester?"

"Nobody's fool."

589   Sign in a beachside café

"Shoes are required to eat in the cafeteria."
Then, in pencil, beneath the sign:
"Socks can eat any place they want."

590   Devoted worker

"I always arrive late at the office, but I make up for it by leaving early."

CHARLES LAMB (1775–1834)

591   Unsurprising

Two grizzly bears are walking down the aisle of a supermarket doing their shopping. One turns to the other and says: "Quiet in here today, isn't it?"

592   Anagram

Snooze alarms are made by rearranging the letters:
Alas No More Zs.

593 **Seasons of the heart**

Let the spring in your stride banish the winter in your heart.

594 **It works both ways**

Sometimes happiness makes you smile; but sometimes a smile makes you happy.

595 **A word of warning**

Little Johnny went up to his teacher after a lesson. "I don't want to scare you," he said quietly, "but my dad told me last night that if I didn't get better grades, someone was going to get a spanking ..."

596 **Where am I?**

If someone has a mid-life crisis while playing hide and seek, does she automatically lose because she can't find herself?

597 **Bumper sticker insult**
Oh, evolve!

598 **Point of no return**
"What do you call a boomerang that doesn't come back?"
"A stick."

599 **Almost but not quite**
"I'm not a complete idiot, you know."
"I know, some parts are missing."

600 **Confusion**
If all is not lost, where is it?

601 **Filling a vacuum**
Love is blind, and its seeing-eye dog leaves hairs on the carpet.

602 Touching is believing
Why is it that if someone tells you that there are a billion stars in the universe, you'll believe them; but if they tell you a wall has wet paint, you'll have to touch it to be sure?

603 Leftovers

The things that come to those who wait may be the things left by those who got there first.

604 Are you sitting down?

A witch accidentally transformed her husband into an armchair. He was rushed to hospital, and she called soon afterwards to check his condition. "Comfortable," the nurse told her.

605 Cornish proverb

Laughter and generous giving make a heaven of a crowded room.

606 Happy frog

Time flies when you're having fun. Unless of course you're a frog, in which case a fun time is when you're having flies.

607   **Acrobatics**

A colony of bats, hanging from the ceiling of a cave, discovered a single bat standing upright underneath on the cave's floor. Surprised by this unusual behaviour, the hanging bats said to this maverick in their midst: "Hey, what are you doing down there?"

"Yoga!" the bat shouted back.

608   **Good advice**

Run a mile from the slow to smile.

609   **Mineral-rich**

A man lived for ten years eating only tiny pieces of metal. It was his staple diet.

610   **Incomplete**

I took a night school course with the intention of becoming a wit. But I only got halfway through.

611 **Fruit watch**

Two children were standing in line for lunch. In front of a bowl of oranges there was a sign: "Only take one orange – God is watching!"

The children took one orange each, then moved along to where there was a big pile of chocolate cookies.

"Take as many as you want," whispered one to the other.

"God's watching the oranges."

612   **Signposts**

When choosing a purpose in life, let your heart lead the way and your dreams find the path.

613   **Bus tour**

A couple visiting San Francisco saw a big sign saying "Bus tour, $10," so they thought they'd give it a try. But later they regretted it. "Ten bucks just to take a look around a bus!"

614   **Father and son**

While leaving church one Sunday, little Sammy turned to his father and said, "Daddy, does Jesus go home now too?"

615   **Transformation**

Did you hear about the magic tractor? It went down the road and turned into a field.

616 Crime of passion
Stealing may be grand larceny but stealing a kiss is
just grand.

617 Invisible helpers
How lovely it is to wake up on a summer morning and
see that the fairies have watered the lawn with their
dewdrops.

618 Face time
"Between you and me," said one eye to the other,
"something smells."

619 Answering machine message
"Hello. This is Julia's refrigerator speaking, as her
answering machine has broken. Please will you speak
very slowly, and I'll attach your message to myself with
one of these little magnets."

620 **Mismatch**

Teacher: "Roger, do you know you're wearing one red sock with blue stripes and one blue sock with red spots?"

Roger: "Yes, Miss. And I've got another pair just like it at home."

621   **Secret admiration**

On a visit to Soviet Russia, an American reporter stopped a man in the street and asked him what he really thought of Stalin. The man looked alarmed. He glanced over his shoulder, came up close to the reporter and, once he'd checked that no one was listening, whispered in his ear: "Actually, I rather like him."

622 **Buddhist car sticker**

Om is where the heart is.

623 **Unfair game**

When you're finally holding all the cards, why does everyone else decide to play chess?

624 **Making good**

Two boll weevils grew up in South California. One weevil went to Hollywood and became a famous actor. The other stayed behind in the cotton fields, but never amounted to much. He was the lesser of the two weevils.

625 **Food and drink**

A muffin walks into a bar and orders a beer. The bartender replies, "Sorry, we don't serve food here."

626 Old-fashioned girl
Psychiatrist, to his nurse: "Just tell people we're really busy, OK? Don't keep saying 'It's a madhouse here.'"

627 Hearts and wings
When a kind heart comes smiling, an angel is never far behind.

628 Sheer necessities
I can do without essentials, but I must have luxuries.

629 Tall story
A man tried to smuggle 100 rolls of bathroom tissue out of a store by rolling them around his head. But then again, this may be a turban myth.

630 More! More!
When a clock is hungry it goes back four seconds.

631 **Don't give up!**
Life is an endless struggle full of frustrations and challenges, but eventually you'll find a hairdresser you like.

632 **Talking fashion**
The hat was talking to the scarf. "You hang around here," it said. "I'll go on ahead."

633 **Chatterbox**
I could talk for hours about the pleasure of silence.

634 **Honest answer**

Teacher: "You missed school yesterday, didn't you?"

Pupil: "Not very much, Miss."

635 **Daredevils!**

Men will do anything if there's an element of danger involved. That's why you often find them barbecuing.

636 **Blessings abound**

"What sunshine is to flowers, smiles are to humanity. These are but trifles, to be sure; but scattered along life's pathway, the good they do is inconceivable."

JOSEPH ADDISON (1672–1719)

637 **Consultation**

"Doctor, my hair's falling out, and I wondered if you could give me something to keep it in?"

"How about a paper bag?"

638 **Mind to mind**
Freelance Telepathist wanted. You know where to apply.

639 **Flying turkeys**
The badness of a movie is directly proportional to the number of helicopters in it.

640 **South African proverb**
When dark rain clouds gather, may smiles christen your ark.

641 **To quote that song**
How many roads must a man walk down ... before he admits he is lost?

642 **True but pointless**
On the other hand, you have different fingers.

643 Good karma

"Those who bring sunshine to the lives of others, cannot keep it from themselves."

SIR JAMES M. BARRIE (1860–1937)

644 **Hunger pangs**

"Eat breakfast like a king, lunch like a prince and dinner like a pauper," the old saying goes. And if you're still hungry at midnight, pretend that you're a king who has taken to dressing like a pauper so as to get to know your subjects better. And then make yourself a snack.

645 **Flying high**

A smile is a brand-new feather in the wings that will set you free.

646 **Hopeless me**

I enjoy using the comedy technique of self-deprecation, but I have to admit that I'm not very good at it.

647 **Time for a snack**

Time flies like an arrow. Fruit flies like a banana.

648 **Missing mom**

"Why did the cookie cry?"
"Because its mommy had been a wafer so long."

649 **Heart or chest**

Warm someone's heart today – and I don't mean tip hot soup down their shirt.

650   **On parade**
Did you hear about the karate champion who joined the army? The first time he saluted, he knocked himself out.

651   **Belgian proverb**
Experience is the comb that Nature gives us when we're bald.

652   **Been there, done that ...**
You know, when you've seen one shopping centre you've seen a mall.

653   **Dotty dialogue**
A polar bear walks into a bar and says to the bartender, "I'll have a gin .... and tonic."
The bartender asks, "Why the big pause?"
The bear says, "I dunno, I've always had them."

654 Subterfuge

The easiest way to get a child's attention is to sit down with the paper and look comfortable.

655 Thirsty work

How much deeper would the ocean be if it didn't contain any sponges?

656 Even so

"Your friend is the man who knows all about you, and still likes you." ·

ELBERT HUBBARD (1856–1915)

657 Robin and Marian?

Just think – if marriage were outlawed, only outlaws would have in-laws.

658 **Desperate measures**

Why do we press harder on our TV remote control when we know the batteries are flat?

659 **Perfect presents**

There is nothing so beautiful among all the gifts that one human being can offer another than a simple, heartfelt smile.

660 **Cowboy saying**

Don't squat with your spurs on.

661 **Girls look out!**

See no evil, hear no evil, date no evil.

662 **Dangerous beast**

"What do you call a one-eyed dinosaur?"
"Doyouthinkhesaurus?"

663   **Teaching by example**

We have a lot to learn from dogs – for example: running to greet our loved ones when they arrive home; never turning down the chance for a long walk; taking frequent naps and stretching when we wake up; and recognizing that when someone is having a bad day, the best thing to do is sit quietly near them, just so they know you're there.

664   **In praise of tickling**

"'Tis a good thing to laugh at any rate; and if straw can tickle a man, it is an instrument of happiness."

JOHN DRYDEN (1631–1700)

665   **In the know**

An expert: Someone who knows more and more about less and less, until finally he or she knows absolutely everything about nothing.

666   **Deep in the jungle**
Why doesn't Tarzan have a beard?

667   **Balkan proverb**
A good rest is half the work.

668   **Feline foibles**
"Cat: A pygmy lion who loves mice, hates dogs and patronizes human beings."
OLIVER HERFORD (1863–1935)

669   **Self-adhesive**
Why doesn't glue stick to the bottle?

670 **Laugh lines**

"Wrinkles should merely indicate where smiles
have been."

MARK TWAIN (1835–1910)

671 **Amphibian**

"What do you do if you see a blue frog?"
"Stop and cheer him up."

672 **Around the table**

A meeting is an event at which minutes are kept and
hours are lost.

673 **Caring approach**

How many psychologists does it take to change a light
bulb? Just one, but the light bulb really has to want
to change.

674 **That doggy in the window**
Did you ever notice that when you blow in a dog's face he doesn't like it, but when you take him for a ride in the car, he sticks his head out of the window?

675 **Nigerian proverb**
Hold a true friend with both your hands.

676 **Outside the law**
An atheist can't find God for the same reason that a burglar can't find a policeman.

677 Do it yourself
Delegation is a sign of weakness. Leave it to someone else.

678 Walking on air
Laughter gives hope its wings.

679 Latest look
Look at that tourist with a camera around his neck. Is that what people mean when they talk about a snappy dresser?

680 **Notice in a window**

Out of my mind. Back in five minutes.

681 **Plus and minus**

Two atoms are walking down the street.
The first one says, "Oh no, I just lost an electron!"
The second one says, "Are you sure?"
And the first one replies, "I'm positive!"

682 **To err is human**

"A life spent making mistakes is not only more
honourable but more useful than a life spent doing
nothing."

GEORGE BERNARD SHAW (1856–1950)

683 **Slicked back**

"Why do bees have sticky hair?"
"Because they use honeycombs."

684   **En route**

I don't mind going nowhere as long as it's an interesting path.

685   **World on loan**

"A true conservationist is a man who knows that the world is not given to him by his father but borrowed from his children."

JOHN JAMES AUDUBON (1785–1851)

686   **Riddle-di-dee**

"What goes tick-tock bow-wow?"
"A watchdog."

687   **Just to be sure**

The best way to keep kids at home is to make sure the home has a pleasant atmosphere ... and let the air out of their tyres.

688   Higher animals

"An evolutionist is someone who believes that human beings are a species of monkey."

FROM A HIGH SCHOOL STUDENT'S ESSAY

689   New moon

"How does a man on the moon get his hair cut?"

"Eclipse it."

690   Two of us

Do not walk behind me, for I may not lead. Do not walk ahead of me, for I may not follow. Walk beside me and be my friend.

691   Mature gratitude

There is always something to be thankful for if you take time to look for it. For example, I am sitting here thinking how nice it is that wrinkles don't hurt.

692   Ego trip

An example of delusions of grandeur: going to a
fancy-dress party as yourself.

693   Musical torture

A missionary was travelling in Africa with his guide. In
the distance they heard drums. "What do those drums
mean?" the missionary asked nervously. The native
replied, "Drums OK, but if they stop – very bad." They
walked on, then suddenly the drums stopped. In panic,
the missionary asked, "What happens now?" The guide
crouched down, covered his ears with his hands, and
answered with a groan of despair, "Tuba solo."

694   Flood lovers

"When Noah built the ark all the seahorses took a
rain check."

GERRY, AGED 9

695   **Fond farewell**

"What does a buffalo say when her son leaves home?"
"Bi-son."

696   **Lost among words**

Two trucks loaded with thousands of copies of *Roget's Thesaurus* collided as they left a New York publisher's warehouse last Wednesday. According to news reports, witnesses were stunned, startled, aghast, taken aback, amazed, stupefied ...

697   **Spellbound**

I was once in a spelling bee, but I lost because the other contastents cheeted.

698   **English proverb**

Every path has its puddle.

699   Them and us

"We always like those who admire us; we do not
always like those whom we ourselves admire."

FRANÇOIS DE LA ROCHEFOUCAULD (1613–1680)

700   Professional job

Dad: "I need to fix a dent in the car."

His son, aged 4: "Why don't we go to the dentist?"

701   Cat skills

Behind every gifted woman there is often a rather
talented cat.

702   It can't be done

Before claiming that something is impossible, we
should ask ourselves whether we are simply making an
excuse for our own unwillingness.

703 **Newsworthy**

Want to trace your family tree? Run for public office or win the sweepstake.

704 **No appeal**

Now I know why they call them trial lawyers. I tried one and I didn't like him.

705 **A day at the zoo**

A father took his young son to the zoo for the day. "Did you and Daddy have a good time?" asked the mother when they came home. "Yes," replied the little boy. "Daddy particularly enjoyed it when one of the animals came in at 33 to 1."

706   **Anatomy lesson**
A man should be greater than some of his parts.

707   **Underwater**
"What lies on the bottom of the sea and shakes?"
"A nervous wreck."

708   **How to make an impact**
"Always do right. This will gratify some people and
astonish the rest."
MARK TWAIN (1835–1910)

709   **German proverb**
God gives us nuts but He does not crack them.

710   **Thank you so much**
True gratitude is so much more than the secret hope of
further benefits.

711   Kith and kin

A father spent ages explaining to his little girl that Roger, his son by his first wife, was her half-brother. When Roger visited, the girl stared at him long and hard and finally whispered, "Where's the other half?"

712   Name that animal

"What do you call a deer with no eyes?"
"No eye-deer."

713   Basically sound

It's OK to be slightly cracked, so long as you are basically a good egg.

714   No losers

A cake can be divided in such a way that each recipient thinks they are getting the biggest piece: this is the art of compromise.

715   C&W

"What do you get if you play a country music
song backwards?"

"You get your wife, dog, truck and job back."

716   Friends in need

When we offer advice to friends, it's all too easy for us
to fall into the trap of trying to please them rather
than to help them.

717   Never alone

Good friends are like stars – you can't always see them
but you know they're there.

718   The great and the good

A good leader inspires others with confidence in him;
a great leader inspires others with confidence in
themselves.

719 Overheard in a gallery

Art gallery curator: "The still-lifes here are amazingly realistic. I recently had to offer one guy some of my chocolate to stop him grabbing at the apples."

720 Once bitten

"What do you call a lion trainer who puts his right arm down a lion's throat?"
"Lefty."

721 Faulty calendar

"Which are the strongest days of the week?"
"Saturday and Sunday. All the rest are weak days."

722 Quick!

He who laughs last thinks slowest.

723 Priorities

If you think you can't live without something, you're probably wrong – unless it's your alimentary canal or your central nervous system.

724 **Divide and conquer**
Five out of four people have trouble with fractions.

725 **Set sail**
The ship is safer in the harbour, but it is not built for that.

726 **Dress sense**
"What do you call it when someone attaches a clock to their belt?"
"A waist of time!"

727 **Owning up**
We are all much more likely to admit to poor memory than to poor judgment.

728   Smart answer

Children's questions can open adult eyes to the wonders of the world – and teach you to be creative in your answers. When they ask things like "Why is it raining?" you can say that God is crying. But if they ask why, resist the temptation to answer, "Because you threw your orange juice all over the kitchen floor."

729   Japanese proverb

Fall seven times, stand up eight.

730   Charity begins at home

A little girl asked her mother for some money to give to the old lady in the park. The mother was touched by the little girl's kindness and gave her the money she asked for. "Tell me," said Mom, "'why is she so poor? Is she not able to work?"

"Oh yes," replied the little girl. "She sells ice cream."

731   Double the trouble

"What are good names for identical twin boys?"

"Pete and Repeat."

732   In the wee small hours

If you lie awake at night worrying, worry only about the mysteries of the cosmos, not about love or money.

733   Prime spot

We can live our life perfectly successfully even while following false principles – like the fisherman who always fished under a bridge where the trout congregated to take shelter from the rain.

734   Hybrid

"What do you get when you cross a cockerel, a poodle and a ghost?"

"Cockapoodleboo!"

735 $MXVIII

Fight back! Fill out your tax forms in Roman numerals.

736   Harmless

"What kind of robbery is least dangerous?"

"A safe robbery."

737   Go for it!

The wise do not give up gracefully: if the ink in their pen runs dry, they immediately grab a pencil.

738   Time warp

"It's a poor sort of memory that only works backward."

LEWIS CARROLL (1832–1898)

739   Wild and woolly

"Where do sheep get a hair cut?"

"At the baa baa shop!"

740   **Just when you need it**
A little help at the right time is better than a lot of
help at the wrong time.

741   **The art of the real**
A carelessly planned project will take three times
longer than expected; a carefully planned project will
only take twice as long.

742   **Shock tactics**
"To obtain a man's opinion of you, make him mad."
OLIVER WENDELL HOLMES (1809–1894)

743   **Parents' plays**
Isn't it strange – we spend the first twelve months of
our child's life waiting for them to walk and talk, and
the next few years trying to get them to sit down and
be quiet.

744 **Fitting in**
A woman joined a yoga class and told the teacher she wanted to learn the lotus position.
"How flexible are you?" the instructor asked.
"Well, I can't make Thursdays."

745 Consolation

Everything is OK in the end. If it's not OK, it's probably not the end.

746 Bankside hero

"My dad's a great fisherman to the top of his waders. Above that he might as well be trying to catch atoms."

JOSHUA, AGED 11

747 Strong stuff

"A good statue can be rolled downhill without causing any damage."

MICHELANGELO (1495–1564)

748 Stuck in your ways

Ideas should be well-treated guests, not permanent housemates. When they start turning up at your door with their own furniture, it's time for some serious self-questioning.

749 Be prepared

Always carry a bowl, in case it rains soup.

750 Hush!

"Why did the doctor tiptoe past the medicine cabinet?"
"Because she didn't want to wake the sleeping pills!"

751 One hump or two?

It is easier for a camel to pass through the eye of a
needle than it is to break its back with a straw.

752 Bare bones

"Why didn't the skeleton go to the dance?"
"Because he had no body to go with!"

753 No guarantee

"As a matter of fact" is an expression that precedes
many an expression that isn't.

754 Danish proverb

Bad is never good until worse happens.

755   Kids with character

It's a characteristic of normal children that they don't act that way very often.

756   Placebo

"The art of medicine consists in amusing the patient while nature cures the disease."

VOLTAIRE (1694–1778)

757   First aid check

A Good Samaritan went up to a little boy who slipped on the ice. "Are you OK?" she said. "You should have two of everything on the sides and one of everything in the middle."

758   Look inside

If your living room window is dirty, you don't go out to polish the view!

759 **Straight As**
I passed my ethics exam.
Of course, I cheated.

760 **Walking on eggshells**
A diplomat is a person who thinks twice before saying nothing.

761 **Morning after**
"Let us have wine and women, mirth and laughter,
Sermons and soda-water the day after."

LORD BYRON (1788–1824)

762 **Revealing ourselves**
We never disclose our character so clearly as when we describe another's.

763   **Toward midnight**

"Why was Cinderella such a bad baseball player?"
"Because she had a pumpkin for a coach ... and she ran away from the ball."

764   **My hero**

When confronted by a difficult problem you will usually be able to solve it more easily if you reduce it to this fundamental question:

"How would the Lone Ranger handle this?"

765   **Shhhhh!**

A universal law of etiquette says the mouth is the only part of the body that's allowed to make noises in public.

766   **Aiming high**

"Why are mountain climbers curious?"
"They always want to take another peak."

767 Hebrew proverb

If one person tells you that you have the ears of an ass, pay no attention. If two people tell you this, go get yourself a saddle.

768 Results count

On the difference between men and women: the cock may crow but it's the hen that lays the egg.

769 Don't gamble

A bookmaker is a pickpocket who lets you use your own hands.

770 Good deeds

"When a friend is in trouble, don't annoy him by asking if there is anything you can do. Think up something appropriate and do it."

EDGAR WATSON HOWE (1853 1937)

771 Paranoia

You can learn a lot about paranoid people just by following them around.

772 Impasse

A person who can't lead and won't follow makes an effective roadblock.

773 Stay active

Footprints on the sands of time are not made by sitting down.

774 Keep learning

"The recipe for perpetual ignorance is:
be satisfied with your opinions
and content with your knowledge."

ELBERT HUBBARD (1856–1915)

775   A woman's world

Eve was created for the garden of Eden because God was worried that Adam would get lost in the garden and, being a man, would never ask for directions.

776   A question of numbers

"What have you got if you have eight oranges in one hand and five in the other?"
"Big hands."

777   African proverb

An army of sheep led by a lion would vanquish an army of lions led by a sheep.

778   Killjoy

"What's the best way to attack a circus?"
"Go for the juggler."

779 **All excited**
Dogs make terrible poker players. Whenever they get a good hand, they wag their tails.

780 **Proverbial wisdom**
A bird can sing with a broken wing, but you can't plume a hat with a frog.

781 **Tree of life**
It's OK to go out on a limb – that's where the fruit is.

782 **Brute force**

Muscle power alone solves very few problems, though it's handy when you get your toe stuck in the bathtap.

783 **High price**

Letting people make you angry is not a good idea. It may force you to go on an anger management course, and that's usually very expensive.

784   Ego trip

Beware the man who has never said an unkind word –
it may be because he's always talking about himself.

785   Travel talk

"We are all travellers in the wilderness of this world,
and the best we can find in our travels is an honest
friend."

ROBERT LOUIS STEVENSON (1850–1894)

786   Raising the bar

Exceeding people's expectations has the unfortunate
effect of raising them for the next time.

787   Thank goodness!

"What's the greatest invention there has ever been?"
"Venetian blinds. If it wasn't for them it would have
been curtains for all of us."

788 Naming by numbers

I'm the fifth child in my family. My parents heard that one in five people in the world is Chinese, so when I was born they named me Shen Mei.

789 Snake cure

A phobia about snakes can easily be overcome by the two-step acclimatization programme. Paint a length of rope in yellow and black stripes and wear it around your waist for a week in place of a trouser belt. Then apply to the local zoo ...

790 Right and wrong

The right to bear arms is only slightly less ludicrous than the right to arm bears.

791 Turkish proverb

Even a stopped clock is right twice a day.

792 Congratulations!
Happiness is when you can congratulate yourself on your uncanny skill in dressing for today's weather, not yesterday's.

793 Two gold rings
"How much did the pirate pay for his earrings?"
"A buccaneer."

794 Please release me
Smiling opens up a stranger's treasures; frowning keeps them under lock and key.

795 **Beware of the banker**

"A banker is a fellow who lends you his umbrella when the sun is shining and wants it back the minute it begins to rain."

MARK TWAIN (1835–1910)

796 **How to get by**

The only substitute for good manners is fast reflexes.

797   Lead us not into temptation

A Sunday School teacher was discussing the Ten Commandments with her five and six year olds. After explaining the commandment to "Honour thy Father and thy Mother", she asked: "Is there a commandment that teaches us how to treat our brothers and sisters?" One little boy piped up, "Thou shall not kill."

798   The thought that counts

Mom: "Why did you look so disappointed when Aunt Trudy gave you a pocket calculator for your birthday, David?"
David: "Because I already know how many pockets I have."

799   Squawk!

"What's orange and sounds like a parrot?"
"A carrot."

800 **Silence is golden**

If something goes without saying, let it.

801 **New look**

"What wears a coat all winter and pants all summer?"
"A dog."

802 **Letting your hair down**

If you're not embarrassing your teenagers, you're obviously not enjoying yourself.

803 **Who dares wins**

The early bird may catch the worm, but it's the second mouse that gets the cheese.

804   Always late

Experience is something you don't get until just after the first time you need it.

805   Public service

Wouldn't it be nice if you could call Information and ask them where you left your keys?

806   Cupid's clothing

If love is blind, why is lingerie so popular?

807   Downtown

Anyone who says money can't buy happiness just doesn't know where to shop.

808   Oh well!

People who say we should all pay our tax bills with a smile are wrong. I tried it, but they insisted on cash.

809   **The watch word**

In philosophy one classic argument that proves the existence of God is known as the "watchmaker" argument. If you come across a watch, carefully designed with intricate parts that all relate to each other, you know that it owes its existence to a watchmaker. Our world, similarly, is cleverly designed, with one part dependent on another. Someone must have made it. The burning question is: is it still under guarantee?

810   **Hot and cold**

The English language is strange – skating on thin ice can get you into hot water.

811   **Magic interlude**

Life's golden age is when the kids are too old to need baby sitters and too young to borrow the car.

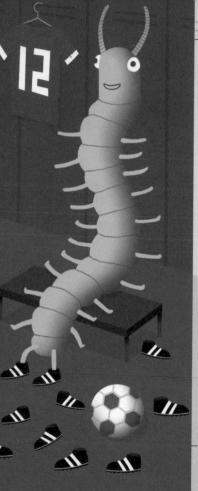

812 Feeling bored?
If you feel that life is
not presenting you
with enough
challenges, try
mending a broken
umbrella.

813 Skipping school
People who think the
world revolves
around them
must have been
home sick with dizzy
spells when the
solar system was
taught at school.

814 **Booting up**

In the animal soccer match, a centipede was brought out for the second half and scored 10 goals, winning the match. "Why didn't you bring him out in the first half?" a reporter asked. "Well, we wanted to," replied the manager, "but it took him an hour to put his boots on."

815 Compulsory training

Mother: "Are you stealing your little sister's candy?"
Daughter: "No, Mommy. I'm helping her to share."

816 Praise indeed

Don't expect to be congratulated for doing nothing.
Not even a mosquito gets a slap on the back until it
starts work.

817 Loving bond

Your children know you love them by your presence,
not your presents.

818 Character flaws

If people's faults were written on their foreheads,
barbers would be bankrupts and long hair would be
back in fashion.

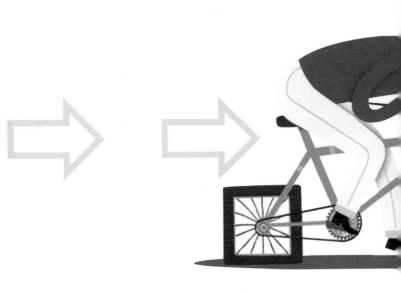

819 **Extra time**

Every hour you spend exercising is an hour added to your life. But what's the good of that extra time if you spent it on exercise?

820 **Getting serious**

When the going gets tough, time to put neater knots in your shoelaces.

821 **Name check**

"I'm very glad you called me Emily," said the little girl to her mother.

"Why's that, dear?"

"Because that's what all the girls at school call me."

822 **Seal of approval**

"When a man's willing and eager, the gods join in."

AESCHYLUS (525–456BC)

823 **Good companions**
Make friends with pagans: they'll worship the ground you walk on.

824 **Keep smiling**
Whatever you do, don't frown. Who knows who might be falling in love with your smile?

825 **Live longer**
He who laughs, lasts.

826 **Grand assumption**
Said the vain writer who had sent his book to a friend: "Tell me, how did you love my novel?"

827   Morning glory

Did you hear about the boy who sat up all night wondering what had happened to the sun? Finally, it dawned on him.

ALASDAIR, AGED 9

828   Everyone is welcome

Anyone who comes within three yards of us is on our home ground. Treat them as a guest. Lavish hospitality. Be generous, as a host should be. Make sure that they'll enjoy coming again.

829   School trip

A mother was asking her son and daughter what they were going to do at school that day. "We're having a quiz on the moon," answered her daughter.

"Are you going to let her go?" asked the little boy.

830   Whirlwind romance

"I am not in favour of long engagements. They give people the opportunity of finding out each other's characters before marriage, which I think is never advisable."

OSCAR WILDE (1854–1900)

831 **Heard but not seen**

The invisible man and the invisible woman got married
– their children were nothing to look at.

832 **Proverbial wisdom**

Love lives in cottages as well as in courts.

833 **Real exchange**

If only we can master the art of thinking continually
while talking and listening alternately, a whole world
of wonder opens up – the joy of true dialogue with
another soul.

834 **Floral tribute**

Blossoms tickle the fancy, flowers seed in the soul.

835 **More than skin deep**

True beauty is nothing but the halo of happiness.

836 **The incredible shrinking man**

A man rushed into the doctor's office and shouted, "Doctor! I think I'm shrinking!"

The doctor replied soothingly: "Now, settle down. You'll just have to be a little patient."

837 **Astronomy**
A new moon is the night sky smiling sideways.

838 **Abyssinian proverb**
The whisper of a pretty girl can be heard further than the roar of a lion.

839 **Hello hello!**
A sincere greeting splashes sunshine over the soul.

840   Showdown

There was a guy telling his friend that he and his wife had a serious argument the night before.

"But it ended," he said, "when she came crawling to me on her hands and knees."

"What did she say?" asked the friend.

"She said, 'Come out from under that bed, you coward!'"

841   Jail break

There was a break at the prison yesterday. An ex-fortune teller, described as being very short, broke out of prison. The public is advised to be on the lookout for a small medium at large.

842   Proverbial wisdom

Never sell the skin till you've caught the bear.

843   **Never mind!**

"What do you say to an elephant that won't let you on its back for a ride?"

"Forget it."

844   **Dream on**

Keep your head in the clouds … you'll be the first to know when it rains, and in the best position to see the silver lining.

845   **Virtuous circle**

Be good to a friend and a friend to good.

846   **Digital dialogue**

Jason, aged 6, was watching the cursor flashing on his father's computer screen. "Look, Dad!" he said. "The computer's winking at me!"

847 **Tree party**

Hug a tree! It will teach you the value of strength and endurance – by remaining completely silent when you ask it to lend you $100, massage your neck, or give you a lift to the shopping mall.

848 Be fair

"Abuse a man unjustly, and you make friends for him."

EDGAR WATSON HOWE (1853–1937)

849 Loose schedule

Note on a door: "Out to lunch; if not back by five, out for dinner also."

850 Persian sunrise

"The breeze at dawn has secrets to tell you. Don't go back to sleep."

JELALUDDIN RUMI (1207–1273)

851 More to do

A little girl comes home after her first day at school.

"So," asks her mother, "what did you learn?"

"Not enough." replies the little girl. "They want me to go back tomorrow."

852   Datelines

A boy was about to go on his first date, and asked his father for advice on what to talk about. His father replied: "My son, there are three subjects that always work: food, family and philosophy."

The boy picked up his date and soon found himself at a loss. He remembered his father's advice, and chose the first topic, asking the girl: "Do you like pancakes?" She said "No," and the silence returned.

After a few more uncomfortable minutes, the boy tried the second subject. He asked, "Do you have a brother?" Again, the girl said "No," and again, silence.

The boy then played his last card. He thought of his father's advice and asked the girl: "If you did have a brother, would he like pancakes?"

853   Important sign

Do not throw stones at this notice.

854 **A toast**

May your pleasures be as deep as the ocean, may your sorrows be as light as the foam.

855 **Urgent business**

Opportunity may knock once, but temptation leans on the bell.

856 **One last party**

Eat, drink and be merry – for tomorrow we diet.

857 **Circulation route**

"Blood flows down one leg and up the other."

JANICE, AGED 8, IN A BIOLOGY CLASS

858 **Come out of your shell**

Consider the turtle: it can't go anywhere unless it sticks its neck out.

859 **Go with the flow**

Don't let your worries get the better of you – remember, even Moses started off as a basket case.

860 **Workers of the world**

Why is it that people who spend their day sitting down often earn more money than people who spend their day working on their feet?

861 **A question of gravity**

"Does a grub feel dizzy when the apple it lives in falls off the tree?"

ELIZABETH, AGED 9

862 **Escape clause**

"It is impossible to enjoy idling thoroughly unless one has plenty of work to do."

JEROME K. JEROME (1859–1927)

863 **A taste of honey**
"Pleasant words are like a honeycomb, sweetness to the soul and health to the body."
PROVERBS 16:24

864 **Conundrum**
Why isn't "phonetic" spelled the way it sounds?

865 **Irish proverb**
A good laugh and a long sleep are the best cures in the doctor's book.

866 **A numbers game**
Be nice to other people:
remember, they
outnumber you several
billion to one.

867 **The four best things about getting older**
There is nothing left to learn the hard way.

868 You can have a party and the neighbours don't
even know you're having it.

869 You can sing along with elevator music.

870 Your secrets are safe with your friends because
they can't remember them either.

871 **Character clue**

You can tell a lot about a person by whether or not they have ticklish feet.

872 **Yiddish proverb**

What soup is to the body, laughter is to the soul.

873 **Roads blocked**

How does the guy who drives the snowplough get to work?

874 **Beyond influence**

Pay attention to the weather and you might learn something: it is completely unmoved by criticism.

875 **Workout**

Laughing is great exercise – it's a bit like an inward form of jogging.

876 Get weaving

"The bird a nest, the spider a web, man friendship."
WILLIAM BLAKE (1757–1827)

877 Shell shock

The human cannonball decided to leave the circus.
"You can't quit," said the circus master. "Where will I
find another man of your calibre?"

878 Chinese proverb

There is no economy in going to bed early to save
candles if the result is twins.

879 You're a star!

"If I could reach up and hold a star for every time
you've made me smile, the entire evening sky would
be in the palm of my hand."
ANONYMOUS

880 **Don't worry**

It's OK to be nobody. Nobody's perfect.

881 **Things are looking up**

"We shall find peace. We shall hear the angels, we shall see the sky sparkling with diamonds."

ANTON CHEKHOV (1860–1904)

882 **Photo call**

A little boy was showing his grandmother a photo album. They came to a particularly nice photo of him.

"That's a lovely photo," said the grandmother.

"Mother doesn't think so," replied the little boy. "She keeps saying she wants to get it blown up."

883   Art lesson

If you buy felt-tip pens for your children it'll make your kin scrawl.

884   Porky goes quiet

"What do you call a pig who's lost his voice?"
"Disgruntled."

885   Two laws

Murphy's Law: If something can go wrong, it will.
Cole's Law: Thinly sliced cabbage.

886   Chinese proverb

When you have only two coins left in the world, buy a loaf of bread with one and a lily with the other.

887   Cash on demand

Madness takes its toll. Please have exact change.

888   **Telling detail**

There is a theory that the 1969 moon landing, when men stepped onto the moon for the first time, was a fake staged in a studio and hushed up by NASA. It isn't so much the double shadows that give us a clue as the signpost saying "Earth 384,400 miles".

889   Night visitors

Fireflies are actually Martian spacecraft keeping their headlights on for as long as they dare.

890   Safe journey!

As you slide down the banister of life, may the
splinters never point the wrong way.

891   Smart choice

A hippo does not have a sting in its tail, but a wise
man would rather be sat on by a bee.

892   Strategic thinking

"Always acknowledge a fault frankly. This will throw
those in authority off their guard and give you the
opportunity to commit more."

MARK TWAIN (1835–1910)

893   Looking back

The good old days ... when everything was in black
and white and you could buy a house for the price of a
bag of candy.

894   Options

It was mealtime on a small airline and the flight
attendant asked the passenger if she would like dinner.

"What are my choices?" she asked.

"Yes or No," came the reply.

895   Find your rhythm

"Those move easiest who have learned to dance."

ALEXANDER POPE (1688–1744)

896   Blood supply

A teacher was giving a lesson on the circulation of the
blood. Trying to clarify things, she said, "Now, class, if
I stood on my head, the blood would run into it, and I
would turn red in the face. But why is it that while I'm
standing upright in the ordinary position, the blood
doesn't run into my feet?" One little girl shouted out,
"Cause your feet ain't empty!"

897 **Angels like us**
Angels watch over us. They might occasionally get distracted by a big football or baseball game, but they'll always come back to us in the end.

898 Self-esteem

There was once a man with such an inferiority complex that whenever he stepped into an elevator he asked the bellboy to take him up to the floor he wanted "so long as it isn't out of your way".

899 Level speaking

"He who truly knows has no occasion to shout."
LEONARDO DA VINCI (1452–1519)

900 Learn your limits

If you think that you are a person of great influence, try telling somebody else's dog what to do.

901 Japanese proverb

He who travels for love finds a thousand miles no farther than one.

902 In retreat

I don't have a solution – but I admire the problem.

903 Out of bounds

"An abstract noun," the teacher said, "is something you can think of, but you can't touch it. Can you give me an example of one?"

"Sure," a teenage boy replied. "My dad's new car."

904 Delusions

A man went to a psychiatrist, who said to him, "And what's your problem, sir?"

The man replied, "I'm Attila the Hun, I don't have a problem. I have plundered the wealth of empires, my enemies flee before me, my wish is my soldiers' command."

"May I ask why you've come to see me then, sir?"

"It's my wife, she thinks she's Mrs Winterton."

905 **Far out**

If God had intended people to fly, how come he positioned airports so far away from downtown?

906 **Easy wisdom**

Anyone can be wise. All you need to do is think up something really profound and earth-shattering to say, then don't say it.

907 South American proverb
Do not insult Queen
Crocodile until you have
crossed the river.

908 Lost in the desert
"Why did the archaeology student cry?"
"Because he'd lost his mummy."

909 Grow your money
If money doesn't grow on trees, then why do banks
have branches?

910 Anxiety attack
Worry is interest paid on trouble before it's due.

911 Keeping house

My idea of cleaning the house is sweeping the floor with a glance.

912 A rule for life

A boy, frustrated with all the rules he had to follow, asked his father, "Dad, how soon will I be old enough to do as I please?" The father answered immediately, "I don't know. Nobody has lived that long yet."

913 Seasonal spirit

"I will honour Christmas in my heart, and try to keep it all the year."

CHARLES DICKENS (1812–1870)

914 Moms get real

Real mothers know that their kitchen utensils are probably in the sandbox.

915   Praise indeed

"Humour is mankind's greatest blessing."

MARK TWAIN (1835–1910)

916   Sleep thieves

Why is it that people say they "slept like a baby" when babies wake up every two hours?

917   Slow progress

How is it that we put a man on the moon before we figured out it would be a good idea to put wheels on luggage?

918   Overheard in a pet store

A man goes into a pet store and asks for some bird seed. "What kind of birds do you have?" asks the store keeper. "Oh, I don't have any yet," says the customer. "I was hoping to grow one."

919 **Pros and cons**
"Almost every wise saying has an opposite one, no less wise, to balance it."

GEORGE SANTAYANA
(1863–1952)

920   Unexpected

"The secret of humour is surprise."

ARISTOTLE (384–322BC)

921   Ever hopeful

"When we started our new travel agency we wanted a name that would conjure up the carefree pleasures of springtime. So we called it May Travel."

922   Alter ego

"Mommy and Daddy gave me a middle name, to use as a disguise when I want to be naughty."

SALLY JEAN, AGED 6

923   One left, one right

A mother told her son that his shoes were on the wrong feet. The little boy looked perplexed. "They're the only ones I've got," he said.

924   **A course of treatment**
Laughter is the best medicine – and it has no
unpleasant side effects.

925   **Pretty Polly**
A Frenchman with a parrot on his shoulder walks into a
bar. The barman says, "Wow, he's beautiful – where'd
you get him?"
   "In France," says the parrot. "They've got millions."

926   **In days of yore**
"What was Camelot famous for?"
"Its knight life."

927   **In sickness and in health**
"Preserving health by too severe a discipline is a
troubling malady."
FRANÇOIS DE LA ROCHEFOUCAULD (1613–1680)

928 **Tree wisdom**

Hug your local oak. Good things come in trees.

929 **Chinese proverb**

If thine enemy wrong thee, buy each
of his children a drum.

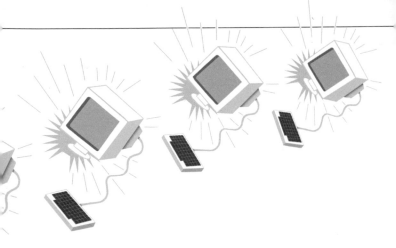

930 **Fighting back**
Your computer may beat
you at chess, but you'll
always be able to get your
own back at kickboxing.

931 Wilt alert

Be suspicious of any doctor whose office plants are in need of attention.

932 Tale of the unexpected

A little girl was typing very fast on her father's computer, telling her father she was writing a story. He asked her what it was about, and she replied, "I don't know, I can't read!"

933 Tooty fruity

You can tell a lot about a person by how ripe they like their bananas to be.

934 Precious metals

Good words are drops of silver; good deeds are buckets of gold.

935 Proverbial wisdom

A new broom sweeps clean, but the old broom knows all the corners.

936 Footware fashion

A man with two left feet walks into a shop and says, "Got any flip-flips?"

937 Feeling better

"After two days in hospital, I took a turn for the nurse."

ATTRIBUTED TO W.C. FIELDS (1879–1946)

938 The beautiful sunset

A reporter was interviewing a 104-year-old woman.

"And what do you think is the best thing about being 104?" the reporter asked.

She gave a simple answer: "No peer pressure."

939   **Bedtime story**

Little boy (frightened of the dark): "Mommy, can you sleep in my room tonight?"

Mom: "No, dear, I have to sleep in the same room as Daddy."

Little boy: "Oh, he's such a scaredy-cat!"

940 **Tough journey**

Two young men were riding a tandem bicycle up a hill, but having a hard time. "I thought we'd never make it," said John on reaching the top. "So did I," said Sam. "A good thing I kept the brakes on, or we'd have slid all the way back down again!"

941 Revenge

A three-legged dog walks in to a Wild West saloon and says: "I'm looking for the villain who shot my paw."

942 Caught cheating

Teacher: "Johnny, I know you copied from Timmy in the last test."

Johnny (sheepishly): "Really? How do you know?"

Teacher: "Well, every time Timmy wrote 'I don't know' in answer to a question, you wrote 'Me neither'."

943 All in the family

Families are like boxes of chocolates – mostly sweet, with a few nuts.

944 Alphabet soup

A man swallowed all the letters from a Scrabble set. The doctor asked him to say "Aaaaa".

945 **Proverbial wisdom**
A reed before the wind lives on, while mighty oaks
do fall.

946 **Insect incident**
A man is walking down the street when he is attacked
by a giant grasshopper, which knocks him out. He
wakes up in hospital, and describes his attack. "Ah
yes," says the doctor, "You're the sixth case we've had
this week. There's a very nasty bug going around."

947 **No time to think**
"A really busy person never knows how much he
weighs."
EDGAR WATSON HOWE (1853–1937)

948 **Grin tactics**
A smile confuses an approaching frown.

949 **Frog watch**

"How can you prove that
a frog has no ears?"
"Yell 'free flies!' and see
if he comes hopping
toward you."

950 **Faint praise**

We like to praise birds for flying. But how much of it is actually flying, and how much of it is just sort of coasting from the previous flap?

951 **Mom and Dad**

As a father's goodness is higher than a mountain, so a mother's is deeper than the sea.

OLD PROVERB

952   Synchronicity
A coincidence is an earthly reply to a cosmic fax you sent earlier.

953   The waiting game
If virtue is its own reward, why do the people who turn up late for a meeting with a friend so often look happier than the friend who's been waiting for them?

954   Solo
I'd like to perform a little number I wrote myself: "Two and a half".

955   Wrapping up
A sweater is something a little boy puts on when his mom feels cold.

956   Pet lore

"What's the difference between dogs and cats?"
"Dogs have owners, cats have staff."

957   Hold that memory

People would enjoy life more if, once they got
what they wanted, they could remember how
much they wanted it.

958   Real clever

Half of being smart is knowing
what you're dumb at.

959   Great gifts

A smile, along with your
word and your heart, is
something you can give away
but still keep.

960   Role play

Two boys were walking home from Sunday School
after hearing a strong sermon on the devil. One said to
the other, "What do you think about all this Satan
stuff?" The other boy replied, "Well, you know how
Santa Claus turned out. It's probably just your dad."

961   **Cat and dog**

Only the most foolish cat would escape a dog by hiding in its kennel; but only the cleverest dog would think to look there.

962   **Vocation**

"Pleasure in the job puts perfection in the work."

ARISTOTLE (384–322BC)

963　No tolerance

"Few things are harder to put up with than the annoyance of a good example."

MARK TWAIN (1835–1910)

964　Raw recruit

A submarine captain was doing his rounds inspecting the new recruits. He came across a young man in the kitchen, peeling onions, crying profusely and swearing to himself under his breath.

"What's the matter, there?" asked the captain.

"My mom's been lying to me all these years," replied the young man. "She says that peeling onions doesn't make you cry if you do it underwater."

965　Laughter cure

"A merry heart is a good medicine."

PROVERBS 17:22

966 **Separate ways**

When teenagers split up, it's like two strips of Velcro®
separating. They make an interesting noise, no real
harm's done, and their function is kept intact.

967 **Cheeky!**

A little boy went to the dentist. The dentist told him,
"You're going to have a filling today." And the little
boy replied, "Can it be chocolate?"

968 **Mealtimes**

Lunch and dinner: two things you can never have for
breakfast.

969 **Number crunching**

Never believe anybody who tries to prove something
with statistics: 83.5 percent of them are completely
made up.

970 **Heavy metal**

I dreamed I was lead guitarist in a rock band ... and woke up to find I'd ripped holes in the knees of my pajamas with my nail scissors.

971   Local lingo

An English tourist in California was telling some locals about her itinerary.

"And that's how I ended up in San José," she said, pronouncing the words as they're spelt.

"Actually, in California we pronounce it San Hosé. How long are you staying?"

"Till the end of Huly."

972   Vital role

A park keeper makes an invaluable contribution to society – you wouldn't believe how many parks have nearly disappeared over the last few years!

973   Forging your destiny

"Opportunity is missed by most people because it is dressed in overalls and looks like work."

THOMAS EDISON (1847–1931)

974   **Home farm**

There's no point in keeping chickens just because you like eggs – you must also have a fondness for feathers.

975   **In stitches**

"Against the assault of laughter nothing can stand."

MARK TWAIN (1835–1910)

976   **Role reversal**

A babysitter is a teenager acting like an adult while the adults are out acting like teenagers.

977   **Twisting an arm**

Diplomacy – the art of letting someone have your way.

978   **Live and let live**

The accepting soul hears others mispronounce *feng shui* yet is unmoved to correct them.

979 **Dog at the Doc's**

"Doctor, Doctor, I think I'm a dog!"

"Take a seat over there please"

"I can't! I'm not allowed on the couch!"

980 **Snow joke**

An Eskimo teacher was teaching some nursery rhymes to her class. "Little Jack Horner," she started to recite, "sat in a corner ..." One little girl's hand shot up in the air at that point. "Please, Miss, what's a corner?"

981 **Proverbial wisdom**

Never test the depth of the water with both feet.

982 **Opportunities**

"Be glad of life because it gives you the chance to love and to work and to play."

HENRY VAN DYKE (1852–1933)

983 **Aiming high**

Reach for the stars. You may not touch one, but neither will you end up with a handful of mud.

984 **Empty-handed**

A hunter goes into a butcher's shop and asks to buy a duck. "Oh, I'm sorry, we're all out of duck, sir. How about a chicken?" "Well, that would be great," says the hunter, "but how am I supposed to convince my wife I shot a chicken?"

985 **On demand**

A pianist is playing the piano in a bar. A customer comes up to him and says: "Do you play things on request?" "Yes." says the pianist. "Terrific! Play cards," says the customer.

986   Timekeeping

"My poor fellow, why not carry a watch?" said Herbert Beerbohm Tree (1852–1917), when he saw a man in the street struggling to carry a grandfather clock.

987   Big and small

To make a mountain out of a molehill is great for the eagle, not so good for the mole.

988 **Good companion**

To tackle loneliness, try enjoying the company of the person you're alone with.

989 **Husband and wife**

"I was a fool when I married you!"

"I know – but I was in love and didn't notice at the time."

990   **Absentee**

The school secretary answered the phone in the office. "I'm sorry," said a deep voice, "but Eddie will not be attending school today as he is unwell." The secretary asked who was speaking. "My father," said the voice.

991   **Electric connection**

Two TV antennae meet and fall in love. The wedding was quite boring, but the reception was great!

992   **Nature's gift**

"Earth laughs in flowers ..."

RALPH WALDO EMERSON (1803–1882)

993   **Seasonal fare**

"What's the most popular Christmas wine?"
"I don't like Brussels sprouts!"

994   Mean molluscs

"Why don't oysters give to charity?"

"Because they're shellfish."

995   Bank account

A man goes into a bank and asks them to check his balance. The teller pushes him over.

996   Elephant whisperer

"I have a memory like an elephant. In fact, elephants often consult me."

NOEL COWARD (1899–1973)

997   Bless you!

"How is a tax bill like a sneeze?"

"You know it's going to happen, and there's nothing you can do about it."

998 Daily tasks

"We should consider every day lost on which we have not danced at least once. And we should call every truth false which was not accompanied by at least one laugh."

FRIEDRICH NIETZSCHE (1844–1900)

999 Making good

A man walks into a pet store and asks for some ants, three mice, a family of cockroaches and 15 spiders.

"What do you need all these for?" the shopkeeper asks. The man answers, "I'm moving out of my apartment this afternoon, and the landlord says I have to leave it exactly as I found it."

1000 Cash flow

Money talks. Mine generally says "Bye!"

1001 Taking a break
Where do forest rangers go to "get away from it all"?

INDEX

Entries refer to page number

A

Addison, Joseph 244
Aeschylus 303
alarm clock 159, 174, 227
aliens 101, 325
Allais, Alphonse 95
angels 85, 193, 196, 241, 322, 329
animals 34, 64, 75, 77, 86, 87, 95, 142, 214, 227, 262, 267, 280, 299, 316
Aragon, Louis 124
Aristotle 340, 357
art 30, 63, 65, 82, 88, 279
Audubon, John James 259

Augustine, St. 133

B

Barrie, Sir James M. 205, 246
bees 13, 17, 144, 218, 258, 326
Belloc, Hilaire 116
Benchley, Robert 93
Bible 38, 128, 171, 199, 204, 261, 294, 318, 358
bicycles 14, 69, 168, 347
Bierce, Ambrose 71, 169
birds 32, 34, 45, 161, 199, 201, 219, 285, 288,

ACKNOWLEDGMENTS

Thanks are due to the many anonymous jokesters who in a spirit of tremendous generosity have launched their inspirations into the public domain, from which many of the "smiles" in this book have descended; and to the following individuals, many of whom have created their own "smiles" as well as picking up some choice ones on my behalf from anonymous sources.

MAIN COMPILERS/WRITERS
Peter Bently, Graeme Grant, Adam Parfitt

OTHER CONTRIBUTORS
Additional "smiles" provided by: Zoë Fargher, James Hodgson, Claire Nielson, David Ross, Bob Saxton, Peggy Vance, Stanley and Oscar Walton and friends, and Wynn Wheldon.